Praise

Pagan Prayer Beads

"Rich in history, creativity, and symbolism, *Pagan Prayer Beads* teaches the reader how to bring spiritual practices of the past into our modern-day lives in a fun, yet inspirational way. Rarely are "how to" books for those who follow a pagan spiritual path so well organized and eloquently written. Clare Vaughn and John Michael Greer are to be commended for their obvious caring and dedication to this work."

— Marcus (Foxglove) Griffin, author of *Advancing the Witches' Craft*

"Is there a pagan alive who doesn't love beads? I'm going to empty my bottomless jar of beads right now and make myself a pagan rosary. Or two or three. What fun!"

— Barbara Ardinger, Ph.D., author of *Pagan Every Day*

"Focusing on both the nitty-gritty details of prayer bead making and the broad scope of their theory and uses, *Pagan Prayer Beads* is a one of those books you'll refer to again and again. Highly recommended!"

— Kirk White, author of *Adept Circle Magic*

"This is a fascinating and comprehensive book packed with information. It is wonderful to find a book that opens up a whole new and meaningful spiritual vista to my own special field of interest."

— Suzen Millodot, author of *Celtic Knots for Beaded Jewelry* and *Chinese Knots for Beaded Jewelry*

Pagan Prayer Beads

Magic and Meditation with Pagan Rosaries

Pagan Prayer Beads

John Michael Greer

and Clare Vaughn

WEISER BOOKS
San Francisco, CA / Newburyport, MA

First published in 2007 by
Red Wheel/Weiser, LLC
With offices at:
500 Third Street, Suite 230
San Francisco, CA 94107

ISBN-13: 978-1-57863-384-5

Cover and text design by Ralph Fowler / rlf design
Typeset in Fairfield Light
Prayer bead photographs by Grey Badger

Printed in the United States of America

Contents

Thanks...

To the redoubtable Patrick Claflin for the
splendid photographs;

To Johnny, muse extraordinaire and
unquenchable rogue;

To Patrick, Mary, Mark, and Lori, our Rogue Valley
family, for endless love and support;

To Jim for sanity, compassion, and recordings of Roethke;

To Peter, whose invaluable friendship ensured that the
Three Realms rosary went beyond the design stage, and for
whom Clare made the very first one.

We couldn't have done it without you. Well, all right, we could
have, but it would have been a much harder task!

Clare's Dedication

To my beloved husband John Michael, without whom, not.

And to my Gods and Goddesses, without whose love,
support, encouragement, challenges, and occasional butt-kicks
I would not have come to write this book.

Pagan Prayer Beads

1

Why Pagan Rosaries?

T HE WORD "ROSARY" conjures up an image of devout elderly women in long black veils telling their beads in the pews of Catholic or Greek Orthodox churches. The phrase "prayer beads" gives rise to thoughts of Buddhist monks, *malas* in hand, chanting the verses of sutras and keeping count by means of their beads. Yet today, as you hold this book in your hands, many American pagans are using rosaries or prayer beads as they pray, meditate, or chant spells.

Rosaries, or strings of prayer beads, originated in India, where *yogins* and *yoginis* were using what is still the standard Hindu *mala* (literally "rose" or "garland") before the 8th century B.C.E. The traditional 108 identical beads of the malas, usually made from the seeds of sacred plants, helped Hindu mystics focus their minds while chanting *mantras*, the sacred syllables of power central to Indian spiritual and magical practice. Buddhist monks and nuns borrowed the mala early on, possibly during the life of the Buddha himself. Buddhist missionaries spread the mala throughout Asia, and, to this day, it remains a fixture of spiritual practice throughout the Far East.

Buddhism also brought the rosary westward. Buddhist missionaries reached Alexandria in Egypt, the intellectual center of the old Mediterranean

world, by the 2nd century B.C.E., and established monasteries throughout central Asia and the eastern parts of what we now call the Middle East. As the newer religions of Christianity and Islam came into contact with Buddhism, they borrowed the rosary as well, though they changed its design to fit their own number symbolism. The Muslim rosary has ninety-nine beads, representing the ninety-nine names of God, and one larger bead representing the deity himself. The oldest Christian rosary has 150 beads, representing the 150 psalms, and is still used today by Benedictine monks. The most common rosary among Catholics nowadays, the fifty-bead Marian rosary, was created by St. Dominic in the early 13th century C.E. after experiencing a vision of the Virgin Mary.

As far as anyone knows, pagan religions in the Western world didn't use rosaries before the arrival of Christianity. Modern pagans recognized a good thing when they saw it, however, and, just like the Buddhists, Christians, and Muslims before them, have adopted the practice and reshaped it to fit the needs of their own faiths. Go to a pagan gathering and you'll find at least one vendor selling beads: a witches' ladder, a Triple Goddess or Full Moon rosary, wrist rosaries for meditation, or rosaries made of specially chosen stones to carry out magical purposes. In the last few years, pagan rosaries have begun to gain popularity, and are now poised to come into their own.

One remarkable difference sets most pagan rosaries apart from their historical predecessors. Hindu, Buddhist, Christian, and Muslim prayer beads usually have a set number of identical beads, with at most one or two specialized beads serving specific functions in prayer, meditation, and ritual. By contrast, most modern pagan rosaries include beads of many different shapes, sizes, and colors, and often have a rich diversity of charms, pendants, and other decorations as well. It's rare to see two pagan rosaries that are exactly alike—and this is exactly as it should be. Modern pagan spirituality values diversity and treasures the uniqueness of the individual, so it's perfectly appropriate that pagan rosaries should be as unique, diverse, and creative as pagans themselves.

Designing a Rosary

Anyone can design and make a rosary suited to their own purposes that encodes their own personal symbolism into a strand of beads and charms. Consider the following examples.

I have just finished making a knotted cord. Starting with a piece of slender woven rayon three feet long, colored a shade halfway between sage green and dark silver-grey, I have, with careful labor and finger-measured distances, created a tool to help me in my work. I wrap the cord three times around my wrist, tucking in the end to hold it securely, and go to my altar to pray. Finally, I remove the cord from my wrist and lay it on my altar in offering. Later, I will begin to use it, passing it through my fingers, counting the knots and silently repeating remembered words. Eventually, there will be a strand of beads, echoing the symbolism of the cord. I will wear that strand as a necklace so that, while I go about my day, I can carry on the work for which the cord was made. Each time my hand strays to my neck and touches the beads, words and images will rise to my mind, fostering prayer and meditation.

Figure 1-1.
Grandma-san's
memorial rosary.

My husband's step-grandmother, Yoshiko, died recently in her mid-nineties. Grandma-san, as John Michael affectionately called her, had an end-lessly warm heart. She adopted him as her own, even though they shared no blood ties. Later, when John Michael and I married, I was added to the list of Yoshiko's grandchildren, and I always loved her dearly. Her death was not unex-pected; she had been slowly declining as her age crept upward. Nonetheless, I felt a strong need to do something to mark her passage and to express my loving sense that she will always be alive in my heart. Given my fondness for beading and her deep love for handicrafts, the obvious solution was to make her a memo-rial rosary. I sorted through my bead box, knowing that I had somewhere, in one of the compartments, some beads she had liked.

After a bit of digging, they surfaced: porcelain cylinder beads, Japanese-made, off-white with a hand-painted blue design of carp. She had smiled over them, pointing to the carp and saying softly, "That's good luck, you know. Long life." She had had a long life, and had done much to be proud of. Clearly, the carp had befriended her. I selected four of the six beads, wanting to leave one or two to bring her memory into another project. In the same compartment was a red porcelain bead—a rounded rectangle, hand-painted with a design of flowers and leaves. She had liked that one too; I remembered her touching it with one finger-tip and murmuring, "Oh, that's pretty." I added it to the others, thinking that the red was a good emblem of the inner fire that had sustained her through the ups and downs of a remarkable life.

None of the other beads in my bead box felt right, so I sat down and spoke aloud to her. "Grandma-san, what do you want in your rosary?" In my mind, I heard her voice suggest—"Maybe blue beads to go with the carp?" OK; but I didn't have any blue seed beads in the right shade. Of course, I was going to need more beads anyway. I planned on making the rosary small and delicate, fit-ting as a memorial for a woman who had been 4'6", but one with only five main beads seemed too small. Off to the bead store I went. There I found two lovely big oval porcelain beads painted with an Imari-style floral design in pink, blue, and a soft green. They went perfectly with the carp. I also found blue seed beads in the right shade.

Figure 1-2.
A rosary for
meditation.

Now something else to balance the red bead? Browsing, I found a small white glass bead shaped like a mouse, with black eyes, ears, nose, and tail. Since I was born in the year of the Rat or Mouse (in Japan they're considered to be symbolically the same), it seemed like the perfect finish, a sort of signature. Then I happened on seed beads of a pale sage green speckled with darker green that perfectly matched the green in the two big beads. I put a bottle of them into my tray, and went to the cash register.

At home, I laid out the beads and finalized a design, imagining Grandma-san looking on excitedly as I worked, just as she would have. Then I set to work with a needle and dark green silk cord. As I strung the rosary, I remembered Grandma-san, her many kindnesses, her warm heart, her soft sweet voice, how fiercely proud she had always been of John Michael and his writing. I often had to stop because tears blinded me, but in the end, the rosary was finished. I hid the knot inside one of the porcelain beads, snipped the thread, and held it up.

Yes; it was right. I blew my nose and took it in to my ancestor altar. There, I called to Grandma-san, told her how much I love her, and offered the rosary to her as a gift from my heart. Then I laid it on my altar, where it remained for a suitable mourning period. Now it rests in a little brocade bag in a drawer below the altar, and whenever I want to remember Grandma-san or seek her advice on something, I pull it out and run the beads through my fingers.

I am under stress. Tired, not sleeping well. Torn about work issues, about money issues, about whether we can afford a planned trip to Britain to visit family, friends, and sacred sites, or whether we will have to cancel. My fingers fumble deep into my bag of rosaries, touch a bead that feels right. I pull, and out comes a rosary of amber glass and rose-quartz beads. I made it for Sucellos, god of sudden change, god of strength. The very feel of the beads comforts and soothes me. I remember being cradled in his arms as he gave me strength to carry me through a difficult time. As I tell the beads, he embraces me again, calling me to rest in his warmth while his arms support me. The beads flow through my fingers. I relax into my god's love and care. The beads flow.

Rosaries for Many Purposes

What purpose can a rosary serve? There are as many answers to that question as there are people who ask it. Of course, rosaries are best known as an aid to prayer and meditation. But they can also be used for relaxation, memory stimulation, and anchoring an energy. Rosaries can be used to carry blessings, to aid in performing spells (especially spells that require repetition of chants or rhymes), to communicate feelings, thoughts, hopes, wishes. They can be talismans, gifts, offerings. A strand of carefully chosen beads and charms can provide a group of symbolic objects to fill your mind and heart with associated images, memories, and thoughts. It can provide a psychological or emotional anchor as you go through a difficult period in your life, whether you are a woman in childbirth, a soldier going off to war, or a recent widower coping with loneliness when the rest of his family lives far away. A rosary made for a special purpose reminds you of that purpose every time you handle it, encouraging you to focus on a goal.

Beyond these practical uses, however, rosaries satisfy something very deep in the human psyche—the need to touch, handle, feel with our fingertips. Your hand contains a higher density of nerve endings than any other part of your body, and your fingertips have the highest density of any part of your hand. We all instinctively pick things up and play with them. Many people do this almost compulsively. Rosaries, strands of beads and charms, are ideal vehicles to fill this urge. They are visually pleasing, with a variety of shapes, colors, and patterns; but they're also pleasing to the touch, providing a variety of textures and surfaces to explore. Caressing an object with an appealing texture provides emotional comfort, stimulates relaxation, and feeds an often-neglected need. In a world where so many tactile surfaces are characterless or unpleasant—styrofoam, laminated composites, cheap harsh paper, plastic—many of us suffer from constant touch hunger.

Figure 1-3. A personal rosary.

Figure 1-4.
A nature-spirit
rosary.

Rosaries can satisfy that hunger. Beads offer tactile surfaces that have a living quality. Stone, wood, metal, and bone caress back when you touch them. The pleasing effect grows with time, making an often-used rosary even more able to provide satisfaction and comfort to the hand. The subtle, unspoken language of touch, by its very nature, forms, strengthens, and renews energy connections; beads take on energy charges as they are handled. These two effects work together in rosaries, turning them into a potent source of beneficial contact. This is part of what makes them such fine tools for prayer and meditation. When your body is quieted by your hand's craving for something to touch, your mind can sink into deeper levels of thought and awareness.

So venture now into the pages of this book and learn how to design, make, and use pagan prayer beads and rosaries to meet your own needs and fulfill your own purposes. A whole world of beauty, magic, and possibility lies within a simple strand of beads. . . .

2

Designing Your Rosary

S o how do you go about designing a strand of prayer beads? There are two basic approaches, with a whole spectrum of variations between them. You can sit and work out a design in an orderly fashion, planning in advance what you want to do and trying to allow for variations in the materials available. Or you can simply open yourself to inspiration and let serendipity be your guide. Of course, since these are just the ends of the spectrum, you can also combine deliberate planning and inspiration according to your own preferences, skills, and talents.

Planned Design

Let's say you want to plan your rosary, at least in its core details, before you go to the bead store. First, decide what the ruling symbolism of your strand will be, then choose the additional elements of symbolism you want to work in.

Sit down and think about who or what you want to honor with the strand, and what materials will be appropriate for your goal. For example, if you are making a rosary for Manannan, focus on colors and materials that will bring sea energies and symbols to the design. This leaves a lot of room for creativity within your chosen symbolism. You can use shell beads, or cobalt-blue glass beads combined with pearlized white-glass seed bead spacers and shell-shaped metal charms, or sodalite beads with their deep-blue matrix and veinings of sea-foam white matched with shell *heishi* spacers. Turn your ideas over in your mind. Explore the possibilities you see, and let new possibilities rise to the front of your mind. Give it a little while to brew, and see what results. If you don't get anything spontaneously, give the process a little nudge.

How do you administer that nudge? That depends on what methods work best for you. People vary in what gets their creative juices going. Workable methods include prayer, meditation, journaling, sketching, walking and thinking, going to the bead store and just looking at what's there, looking through books, doing visualization exercises, incubating a dream, taking a relaxing bath and letting yourself mull over things while you soak, or digging or weeding in the garden. All of these activities let your deep levels of awareness work unhindered and communicate the results of their labors to you. Some people also need to have a stage in the process where they consciously think their way through their goals, often by doing research, making lists, or discussing their project with someone whose feedback they trust.

If your rosary is planned as a gift, have an imaginary conversation or written dialogue with the person in question and see what ideas pop up. The back of your mind may hold a memory or idea that the front of your mind can't reach directly; often, in such cases, a dialogue will bring it forward into the light where you can see it. Such dialogues also provide a voice for your creativity, allowing it to communicate with you in a clearer fashion than hunches and ideas often permit during the busy brainstorming process. Likewise, if your rosary is a memorial for someone who has passed away or left your life, have a dialogue with this person too and see what comes out. You may be startled when a forgotten event returns to memory, or when some small detail you never noticed comes to the fore and becomes important.

If you're making a rosary for a particular deity or deities, go to your altar, light candles, meditate, and pray to him/her/them. Ask for guidance in finding something acceptable. You may receive a direct communication, or you may be answered in subtle ways: a bead out of place in a bin, a clerk putting out new stock as you browse, a sudden shift in mood or feeling as you approach a certain display, a burst of creative energy or ideas leading in a definite direction. The tug of intuition that leads you to a certain store or a certain aisle, the feeling of "let's stop here," the urge to look in that window or wander down this aisle, the stone beads that won't let you go when you'd planned to use glass beads, all may be responses to your prayer. You may also find that some method not listed here is an important way to nudge your own process into action. What matters is to do what works for you.

After you've chosen your basic symbolic frame, decide what numbers, colors, and types of beads you want. This may require a trip to the bead store or a session of Web cruising, depending on how well you know the stock at your supplier. Even if you're not sure what's available, try to get a sense of what you want to achieve. You can always change your goal later to fit the available materials if you can't find exactly what you hoped for. Of course, you may find that there aren't any special colors or numbers you want to use, or any particular type of bead, and that's just fine—the design process includes realizing what you *don't* want or need as much as it does realizing what you *do*. Simply think about what appeals to you in the way of shapes, colors, materials that fit with the symbolism you've chosen.

What if you can't come up with anything definite? Your efforts aren't wasted. The creative process isn't always straightforward, and you've still broken ground on your plan. Your deep mind will be working from the moment you begin thinking the matter over. Even if your ideas are fuzzy, or you seem to have no ideas to speak of, when you arrive at the store you may find that you recognize what you want or need and that, once you have looked over the available beads, you have no trouble knowing which ones to select. Your design may all but make itself, however stubborn it seemed while you were trying to coax an idea into the front of your mind. Trying to sort something out in advance also can help in other ways. If you have trouble finding beads close

Figure 2-1. Three Realms Rosary. Consider how many different
ways these beads could have been grouped.

enough to what you want, you may find that your efforts at planning help you
decide whether something else will do instead, or whether you have to look
elsewhere. If you find that, rather than having trouble finding something suitable, you have several good options from which to choose, it's likely that the
forethought you put into your rosary will allow you to make a clearer and
quicker decision about what will actually suit you best.

Once you find the color, number, and/or materials that you want, calculate
approximately how you want to handle the design. You don't have to nail
down all the fine details yet; just try to sort out basic things like whether
you're going to have sets of beads and how the sets will be patterned. As an
example, take the rosary shown in Figure 2-1. The design Clare settled on
was three groups of nine beads each, grouped according to the realms, with
one charm between each group, and no pendant. However, she could as
easily have chosen to make it nine groups of three, with one bead in each

group from land, sea, and sky, and followed each group of three with a charm, for a total of nine charms. She could also have kept the beads for each realm together in their own group, separated by charms, but within each group separated every three beads by a group of three spacer beads. This would have made each group of nine into three groups of three internally, echoing the larger framing arrangement of three groups. Even a fairly simple design involving nine beads each of three types, in other words, could be carried out in a number of ways, depending on the needs and tastes of the person designing it. In fact, Clare tried all three of the patterns described above, and several others, before settling down to the one she chose. By chance, that was the first design she created for this rosary, but she wanted to examine other options before making a decision. You may want to do this too, or you may hit on an initial design you find perfect for your needs. If you make more than one rosary, you may also find that each is an entity unto itself and that your process for designing and making each is unique. This is quite normal.

Consider two factors deciding how you want to pattern your sets, if you decide to have sets at all: balance and symmetry. These are often treated as inseparable because, normally, something symmetrical is balanced. A good look at Japanese art, however, will quickly tell you that something asymmetrical can be balanced as well. The key to balance is to match emphasis in one place with emphasis in another, the second place being positioned relative to the first in a way that appears balanced to your eye.

Figure 2-2. If you look closely, you'll see that this rosary is asymmetrical.

Balance and Symmetry

- If you are using sets of beads with a demarcating bead or charm between each set, and your design is a simple circlet without pendant, use the same number of demarcating beads or charms that you have sets.

- If you are using sets of beads with a demarcating bead or pendant between each set, and your design includes a pendant, use one more demarcating bead or charm than the number of bead sets you have, because you will need one on each side of the bead that begins the pendant.

- Sometimes a design that is symmetrical without a pendant becomes asymmetrical when you add a pendant. This most commonly happens when you use bead sets with demarcating beads or charms. It can be mended by altering the number of beads in the circlet portion of the design, often by simply adding an additional demarcating bead or charm. (This is another reason to buy one extra of everything.) If you are working with a fixed set of numbers, however, either change the numbers, or omit the pendant, or make an asymmetrical design that retains both the number you want and the pendant. Often, the asymmetry is not particularly noticeable except on close examination.

For example, if you are making an ancestor rosary and use a big, chunky bead low down on the right-hand side of the strand, you can balance that by putting a big chunky bead either low down on the left-hand side (a position that is loosely symmetrical) or high up on the left-hand side (a position that is asymmetrical). Look at the ancestor rosary in Figure 2-3. There is a black wooden hairpipe bead on one side of the strand, about halfway along. This is balanced by a white bone hairpipe in approximately the same place on the other side of the strand. As it happens, both of these are about the same distance along the strand, so are symmetrically balanced. However, if you look closely, you will see a teardrop-shaped stone bead on each side of the strand as well—a pale one on the same side as the bone hairpipe, and a dark one on the same side as the wood hairpipe. These are definitely not in parallel positions; instead, they are asymmetrically balanced.

Notice, as well, that there is no particular order to the smaller beads in Figure 2-3. This was a deliberate choice on Clare's part. For ancestor rosaries, she likes to allow serendipity to govern the order and arrangement of the smaller beads, so she places the larger beads with deliberate spacing and then fills in the gaps between them with smaller beads and charms. The only step she takes to balance these smaller beads is to avoid placing too many beads of the same shape together. If the space between two larger beads is filled with twenty smaller beads—say ten rounds, six disks, and four ovals—she makes sure that these are mixed so that at least some of the disks and ovals are sprinkled among the rounds instead of all grouped together. This is done partly for visual balance; in this type of random design, a mix of shapes appears more balanced to the eye than does a procession of grouped beads with identical or parallel shapes.

It's also done partly to keep the texture of the rosary from being boring and predictable: "Oh, here are all those disks again." Your eyes and fingers are trained to see and accept long sequences of round beads, because that's a normal pattern for beaded jewelry in Western cultures. But longer sequences of other shapes of beads, unbroken by variety, quickly become boring to some

Figure 2-3. Note the beads echoing one another in different sections of the strand.

people. For that reason, in a rosary of mixed-shape beads where the shapes have no symbolic significance, Clare tries to use no more than three in a row of any shape. However, if you like several in a row of some shape, trust your own preferences and do what appeals to you. What bores one person may fascinate another.

What if you want to have exact, or fairly exact, symmetry in your design? That's easy to do. Simply group your beads and charms in some set fashion, based on shape and color. Make every group identical, or make at least the shapes or colors of the beads in every group identical. For instance, look at how the Druid Four Elements rosary (see page 105) is grouped—eight each of four different beads and five charms. The beads in the design were originally all rounds, 10mm in diameter. If you adhere to this original design, you have a design that is exactly symmetrical in terms of shape and length of set, as long as the charms are of about the same size and shape.

If you want an exact symmetry, simply make each group of eight beads all the same color and make the five charms all the same. This will yield a symmetry as exact as it is possible to make without measuring each bead and charm with calipers to make sure they are precisely matched. On the other hand, if you want to stay fairly symmetrical but make it a little less exact, you can make the shapes of the four groups of beads different and keep the sizes the same; use eight 10mm rounds, eight 10mm cubes, eight 10mm twisted squares, eight 10mm flowers. This variation in shape, plus the variation in color suggested in the original design, make for a more interesting rosary, but one that is still balanced to even the most conventional sense of taste. It's a good route to take if you're making a rosary for someone who likes to stay within social bounds, or who has what might be termed a classical sense of taste rather than an avant-garde streak.

On the other hand, if you want balance, but aren't insistent on symmetry, you can vary the shapes of those groups of nine beads quite a bit. In the glass bead Four Elements rosary shown in Figure 2-4, Clare chose to use four completely different shapes of bead: short thick ovals, long thin ovals, saucers, and cubes. This resulted in a rosary whose air and water octads are somewhat long, and whose water and earth octads are somewhat short. To some eyes,

Figure 2-4. The earth and water octads are shorter than the air
and fire octads, but the rosary will still look good.

the strand is not balanced because these octads are asymmetrical, but other
people find the result attractive and balanced.

This is a place where the maxim "To each his own" is appropriate. If you
like asymmetrical designs, great; if you like symmetrical designs, great; both
are possible and you can choose whichever you want. A few brief, simple
rules will help you work out issues of symmetry and balance in your design
process (see sidebars, pages 14 and 18). In the case of this specific rosary, if
you want the lengths of the octads to be more even, add a few extra spacer
beads; the water octad, the shortest of the four, could have two spacer beads
between each blue bead instead of one, for instance. Or you can simply
choose different beads during the shopping phase and size them to match
one another more closely.

If you have chosen no particular parameters of color, number, or material,
see what appeals to you, what's available, and what you think will work for
your needs. See the section on Serendipity (page 23) for pointers on where to
go next. If you have found parameters you want to work within and gotten
them sorted out, see what's available that fits your design. Either way, this is a
good time to check what your supplier has on hand. Make a list of whatever
parameters you have developed, and read chapter 3 on materials for some

Types of Symmetry

- **Hard symmetry:** exactly duplicated beads on both sides; the two sides are mirror images of one another; each bead on the left is matched with another bead of the same size, shape, color, and material placed in the same position on the right, often with a large bead at the center top to mirror the pendant below. Charms are also mirrored exactly.

- **Soft symmetry:** parallel but inexactly matched beads on both sides; the two sides are more or less matched in size, shape, and position, but colors and materials may vary and charms are not exactly matched. The Triple Goddess rosary (see page 121) is an example of soft symmetry.

- **Partial symmetry:** design is based on an even number of charms or accent beads, but some details vary. The Druid Four Elements rosaries in Figure 5-1 (see page 105) are examples of partial symmetry, as is the Ancestor rosary in Figure 2-3 (see page 15).

- **Asymmetry:** design does not consistently match from one side to the other, although some sections may more or less match by chance. The meditation strand in Figure 1-2 (see page 5) is an example of asymmetry.

additional advice on things to think about before you shop. Then head for the store or Web site, list in hand, and take a look. If what you find there seems right for your needs, and your budget is in tune with the prices, go ahead and buy your materials. You'll finalize the last details of your design once you have your materials in hand (see chapter 4, page 75).

You decide you want to give your daughter a strand of prayer beads for her seventh birthday. She has become deeply interested in plants and trees, and is very fond of the legend of the Elder Mother. You want to en-

courage her enthusiasm, and you know the Elder Mother is a potent protector of children. You think about the color of elder: green leaves, cream-colored flowers, and red or purple-blue berries. Red elder is the most common in your area, so you decide to use red instead of blue for the berries.

You consider what else to take into account in developing your design. Your daughter is a very orderly child and has always placed a high value on balance and symmetry, so clearly you want a symmetrical design. She loves to drink elderflower tea, so you decide to try to find beads in approximately that shade of yellow. She loves to wear necklaces, so it might be a good idea to make the strand long enough to fit over her head. You know that, if she likes it, she's going to want to put it on, but you also know that she plays hard enough that a catch or clasp would be likely to break or come undone. It's happened enough times before!

She loves to fiddle with pendants, so you decide to add a pendant and some charms. She's going to be seven, so you start with that as a theme number. Seven yellow beads; six green beads; six cream-colored beads; six red beads—that will be nicely symmetrical for the main circlet of the piece, and can easily be augmented with spacer beads to make it long enough. Then, of course, a seventh bead each of the green, cream, and red for the pendant, ending in some sort of charm. That'll probably work, but you need a bead to tie it together where the main strand meets the pendant. Hmmm; set that aside for now. That, and the pendant charm, can wait until you see what the store has to offer. The rest of the charms, however, are easier; there are a variety of leaves and flowers available, and surely you can find something that will please her. But where to work them in, and how many of them to use?

You sit down with your sketch pad. If you are doing seven of the yellow beads and six each of the others for the body of the rosary, then you can create a sequence of yellow bead – green bead – cream bead – red bead – yellow bead. Although this may have to be altered slightly based on the actual colors, shapes, and sizes of the beads, it does make for a repeatable pattern. With some care in choosing the colors of the beads, it could be very pretty indeed.

Now charms—perhaps six flowers and six leaves, and flank each group of green-cream-red with one flower and one leaf? That would be attractive and provide lots of texture changes for small fingers to play with. Probably gold-toned charms, given the bead colors; silver may not marry well with red and yellow, although a lot will depend on the shades you select. For a pendant charm, perhaps a little gold teacup? It's probably too much to hope for a spray of elderflowers, or a cluster of berries.

You do a basic drawing, roughing out the circlet of beads using simple round shapes, placing a line for each charm, putting in a big circle to represent the spirit bead where the main rosary meets the pendant. Yes; the design is balanced, and you think it will please your daughter's eye as well as excite her, because it relates to her beloved Elder Mother. Time to go bead shopping.

At the store, you quickly find glass beads in the right shade of yellow to represent the elderflower tea. They're a bit bigger than many of the other beads, 12mm twisted cubes, which makes them even better for the role you intend them to play in the design. They'll do a great job of delineating the change from one group of green–cream–red to the next. And their rounded edges will make them comfortable for your daughter's fingers despite their size. You choose eight—the seven you need plus one extra just in case.

Now you turn to the other colors. Some of the 10mm green beads are very close to the shape and color of elder leaves. After some debate, you find one that's right for the design, a flattened oval with faint veins pressed into the surface. Now the red beads are easy, with the leaves there to inspire you; opaque red rounds, also 10mm, catch your eye at once. You grab eight of each. Finally, the cream beads. This isn't as easy; the colors white, cream, and tan are definitely underrepresented in the store's stock, as indeed they are generally. After a bit of hunting, you spot some beads across the store that look as if they're the right color.

They turn out to be 10mm. As a bonus, they're shaped like five-petaled flowers, the shape delicately outlined in gold paint. You compare them with the other beads, and they work in terms of size, shape, and color. They're only available in a strand of twenty-five, which is far more than you need, but, after a minute's consideration, you realize you can use the extras, along with some spacer beads, to make a small bracelet rosary. Your daughter will like that. Satisfied, you turn to the charms.

You find gold leaf charms in a variety of shapes. After a minute of hesitation, you choose six of the one you think is most like the elder leaf. But none of the flowers are really what you had envisioned; the store carries only charms of single flowers, not bunches. And roses and daffodils are a long way from elder. None of the charms representing berries or grapes are a particularly good fit either. Will your daughter be disappointed if she decides the charms aren't just right?

You debate a bit and end up wandering around the store while you think. After all, you still need a bead to bring the circlet together above the pendant, and you need spacer beads and the pendant itself. The latter are easy; you find a seed bead that's mottled in cream and green, the color blend much like that of elder leaves and flowers. And the seed bead's available in size 6/0. As you add a tube to your tray, you think: That's taken care of. But a bead to top the pendant . . .

You wander, looking. On your third circuit of the store, you spot it—a 14mm round bead, cream-colored, engraved with a woman's smiling face. Perfect! It even looks a bit like a drawing of the Elder Mother from one of your daughter's books. You compare it to the other beads, anxiously hoping it'll match. It isn't quite the same cream as the flower beads, but since it won't actually be next to one of them and since it doesn't actually clash, you go ahead and grab it. Big sigh of relief.

Now that brings you back to the issue of charms. Since you can't find flower charms that you're sure will work, you decide on six more of the leaves. Your daughter will still love it.

Finally, with everything else sorted out, you examine the rest of the charms for a potential pendant. Your idea turns out to be a prediction of sorts; the only thing suitable is a little gold teacup, complete with saucer. Luckily, it's the right shape and size to complete the pendant. You've got a rosary, you think, as you put it into the tray with the other beads. You can see it taking shape in your mind's eye. You already have a good strong elastic thread at home on which to string the bracelet, but you need something for the rosary that will take a sudden tug without snapping. You consult with the sales clerk, and she points you to some tough nylon thread. Now you're all set.

At home, you get out your bead tray and lay your purchases in its compartments. Carefully, you lay out the pendant in one of the compartments: the gold teacup, a red bead, a cream bead, a green bead, and, finally, the face bead at the top. You'll go back and add spacer beads as needed once you've got the main circlet settled. Then you begin to lay out the main circlet—seven yellow beads first, widely spaced, filling in the green, cream, and red beads in that order and leaving room for spacer beads.

Now you have one bead of each color left, and the twelve leaf charms. You lay a charm to the right of each red bead, and one to the left of each green bead. The result is very pretty; you're pleased at how well it's working. You insert clear spacer beads into the main circlet until it's large enough to fit easily over your daughter's head, making sure to group the spacer beads in a balanced fashion so she'll like the result. Then you start to insert spacer beads into the pendant.

Whoops! You realize, as you look at it, that there's a teacup, but no bead representing your daughter's beloved elderflower tea. You grab the extra yellow bead, thanking the gods that you bought it so you don't have to make a second trip to the store, and insert it into the pendant design right above the teacup. One spacer bead above the teacup and four more between the other beads, and your design is complete. You start stringing, beginning with a leaf charm that will rest along the back of her neck, making a good place to locate the knot.

Rosary completed, you turn to the bracelet. Ah—here's where you will use the extra green and red beads! You create a pattern of three white flower beads, a green bead, one white flower bead, a red bead, and three more white flower beads. Add spacer beads to make it fit, and you have the perfect bracelet. You string it on the elastic, and hide the remaining eleven white flower beads for some future project—perhaps something you'll teach your daughter to make for herself.

Serendipitous Design

Would you rather simply go to the store and see what calls you, and then base your design around those items? It's certainly possible just to buy the beads that feel right and work out a design using them when you return home. Begin, if this feels right, by saying a prayer at your altar. Meditate for a few minutes about your desire for a rosary, what you want the rosary to mean to you, what purpose you want the rosary to serve. If you draw at all, grab a small sketch pad or a little notepad and a pencil or pen.

Now head for the bead store, pick up a catalogue, or do some Web surfing. If you can, however, actually visit the bead store. It's best to pick up and handle the beads and charms that attract you. With prayer beads, your fingers will tell you more about what works than your eyes will. Regardless of which method you choose, however, the important thing is to open your awareness to anything that direct you to which beads to buy. Follow your aesthetic sense, your personal taste, your hunches and intuitions, you inner perceptions, your attraction to certain animals or symbols or colors, and whatever else may catch your inner or outer eye and say, "Hey! Over here!"

But what if you have absolutely no clue what to look for when you get to the store, and you're worried about being able to find beads to suit your needs? Clare has often seen people who, entering the bead store convinced that they have no idea what to buy and won't be able to find anything suitable, look around for a few minutes and then go directly to beads and/or charms that they later describe as "exactly what I wanted!"

Of course, there are no guarantees that everything will fall into place, but as often as not, the obstacles to your choices will turn out to be technical problems (this clasp is too big and they don't have a smaller one in the same style) or supply shortages (they only have three of these beads left and I want ten) rather than lack of inspiration. So if you have no ideas by the time you get to the store, wander around and look. If necessary, wander around several times. Bead stores are visually busy places and you can miss a lot on your first walk through, or even on your second.

- Belenos, [or any god or goddess you choose to invoke] bright beloved god! Shine upon me and let your light guide me to find what I need to accomplish my purpose. The work of my hands will honor you, and my prayers will turn to you whenever I touch what I have made in your name. I thank you for your aid!

- Ancestors, speak to me and tell me what it is you wish for these beads that I make in your honor. Open my eyes and ears so I may recognize your answer. Give me signs, and I will follow them. I will show you my gratitude and love by offering my work to you when it is completed. Thank you for hearing me!

Still not having any luck? Talk to your deities. Browse some of the beading books and see if you get any ideas. Go have a cup of tea and come back later. Call a friend and ask them to come meet you and offer advice. Better still, if you're feeling low on ideas, ask a friend to go to the bead store with you in the first place—preferably one who knows your tastes well and is familiar with your patron deities and the sort of magical work you do.

If you still can't find anything right, go home and do some journaling; see if something emerges. Trust the process. Sometimes, the first trip just doesn't happen at the right time, or you aren't quite ready yet. Your best bet is to relax. Creativity works in funny ways, and so do the gods. If the first try doesn't work, wait until it feels right to make a second foray, or even a third. You'll get there.

Odds are, however, that you'll find at least a few beads you like on the first visit. It's rare for a trip to the bead store to yield absolutely nothing! After you've selected beads that attract you, look them over and spend a few minutes seeing what options they suggest for a design. Some stores even provide small tables or a section of counter where you can sit and consider your beads in comfort. If you brought a drawing pad, sketch out possible designs, or doodle a little.

Do you think you have what you need? Will the rosary be big or small enough with just these beads? Are you going to want spacer beads, charms, a pendant charm, a few more large beads? What else might fit well with what you have? If you feel as if you have the beads you need, check for stringing materials and anything else you may need to complete the rosary. If you want to get more beads, go back to your shopping.

You may need to repeat this sequence of steps two or three times, possibly during more than one visit to the bead store, when you're doing an unplanned design. As with any other design process, you may run into surprises that move you in a direction different from the one you expected. Sometimes this opens up exciting new possibilities and lets the random factor inherent in serendipitous design bring you to places you might otherwise not have found. A lot of people find this an inspiring, satisfying way to create their own prayer bead strand.

Figure 2-5.
A rosary for Pan.

You want to make a rosary for Pan. You know a lot about his Greek and Roman legends, and the tales spun around him by later cultures, right down to your own time. Pan had no special number that was sacred to him, but he had plenty of symbolism—lord of life, of the wild places, lord of the green chaos that sprawls wherever humanity has not set its taming hand. After offering prayers and incense to him at your altar, you review some of the myths and legends, stocking the front of your mind with their symbols and meanings.

Then you set out for the bead store. This is meant to be an exploratory visit, to locate the various possibilities and take home with you the images of the beads for further meditation, for sketching and design. As you walk, you pay attention to the living world around you, looking for any sign or signal that may hint at what Pan wants. Nothing definite appears, but you find that the sheer variety of shades of green visible in the trees, bushes, grass, ivy, and other plants repeatedly catches at your attention as you pass. You think of Pan's inherent life force, the burgeoning energy you feel whenever he comes to you. Green; a million shades of green. Green seems, more than anything else, to express the feeling you know when the god whose name means All calls to you.

On arrival at the bead store, you head straight for the section of green glass beads. This is one of the biggest sections in the store; a huge variety awaits you. Emerald green, olive green, grass green, the pale singing green of new leaves, the bluish-green of pine needles, a greenish-blue like the waters of your favorite pond, the deep green of cedar boughs, a slightly yellowed green, and many more are all spread out before your eyes. The variety of shapes is almost as great; pressed leaves, simple rounds, long ovals stamped with stars, pony beads, faceted disks, and twisted bicones, each in more than one shade of green, join to hint at a wide range of possibilities.

Praying silently, you try to sort out the visual chaos. You put your eyes into soft focus and wait to see what catches you. After a moment, you realize that a slightly yellowish, slightly olive-y shade of green is grabbing your attention. There's an odd-looking, roughly square bead in that shade; only two of them left, and they almost seem to glow. Well, if there are only two, it's now or never, so you go grab a tray and silently thank the gods you brought your checkbook after all. You take the two square beads and look for what else feels right.

A large bead with shallowly indented sides, neither quite round nor quite square, also seems to have a glow to it. It has a fire-polish sheen of the same green as the other two beads, and it is the only one of its kind. That one comes too. Now the squat, twisted bicones in a clear dark emerald leap to your eye. After some consideration, you decide to get several of these, because it feels as though you'll need more than just one or two. Seven of them go into the bead tray. After that, the pressure on these beads flows away.

Now the field seems to have opened up. Nothing else calls to you specifically, but ten beads, nine of them on the small side, isn't enough for the rosary you want. You start free-associating. A small, faceted bead in a bright pale green reminds you of the beauty of new leaves dancing on the tips of the branches when Indian plum comes out in the spring; three of those. Gold stars painted on a blue-green oval take you back to stargazing through pine branches on your first-ever camping trip; four of those. A fire-polished, grass-green round bead; a couple of silver-lined dark-green pony beads, the lining bringing a beautiful luminescence to their color; some saucer beads of a delicate clear medium green, like leaves seen through water droplets. Each of these finds its way into the tray, in twos or fives or ones, whatever appeals.

Finally, you finish browsing the green glass beads. Great; you have a good selection in the tray now. But this isn't going to be everything. Glass, however beautiful, is a manmade material; you want to include natural materials in a rosary for a nature god! The display case containing the wood, bone, shell, and horn beads is at this same end of the store, just a few feet away. You walk over and take a look. Not shell, since Pan has no ocean connections. You ponder bone, given Pan's associations with wild nature, in which death has a definite place. In the end you decide not to use it, since this rosary seems to need to focus on life energy. You file away the thought of bone for possible future projects, and turn to horn.

Well, there's one possible horn bead—a greenish disk with patterns incised on it—but it just doesn't feel right. And nothing in the wood beads works for you either. You look over the bone beads again, just in case, and feel your original decision was right. Off across the whole length of the store to the display of stone beads, then. Here are aventurine, Chinese jade, moss agate, Siberian jade, green jasper, bloodstone, and many more. Instantly, you know you've found what you want. After examining all of the possibilities, you once again put your eyes into soft focus and wait to see what brings itself to your attention. This time, you find that both the moss agate and the green aventurine have that slight glow to them.

You select several beads of each, making sure they aren't cracked or chipped. Since both stones naturally occur in a range of shades of green, you choose stones that cover that range, from one moss agate bead that is entirely dark green to another that is almost clear with only slight green inclusions, and aventurine beads varying from a pale translucent jade to a deep apple green. Two leopard-skin jasper beads, mottled in bright and dark greens, are also glowing; you take them and put them into the 60-cent compartment of your tray. Now your selection of beads feels complete.

You stop and look at your tray. Hmmm. Charms? A pendant? Maybe. You wander over to that section of the store. No; nothing feels right, nothing looks right, nothing goes with the beads you have. You look over the beads again; yes, these are right. Very well, then, no pendant and no charms. You select some forest-green waxed linen thread for stringing and head for the cash register. While you wait for the customer ahead of you to finish a purchase, you consider the number and type of the beads. It's pretty random, really, which seems just right for Pan; order and pattern aren't really his style. You decide you'll select beads at random as you string, and see if you like the result before you tie the knots and finish it.

At home, you pour the beads into one of the compartments on your bead tray and consider them as you prepare your thread. You decide to use one of the pony beads as the first on the strand, because then, when you finish the rosary, you'll be able to hide the knot inside it. You string the pony bead. You can't put a small bead next to it, since the pony bead has

such a large stringing hole, so you choose one of the twisted bicones in-
stead; they're more than large enough to fit properly. Yes; it works.
Hmmm, now one of the green cubes is grabbing your attention; that next,
followed by a moss agate bead that has rolled away from the others.

Bead by bead, you string the strand, listening to a combination of your
intuition and your grasp of the practical issues, until all the beads are used.
You hold the strand up to examine it. It looks good, and even more impor-
tantly, you can feel Pan's energies in it. After a minute's consideration, you
know you have what you want, and what Pan wants. Smiling, you lower
the strand of beads and begin to tie the finishing knots. Io Pan!

Symbolism

If you choose to plan your rosary in advance, you may decide to put a pattern
of symbolic colors and/or numbers into the design. If you choose serendipity
instead, you can still consider color and number symbolism as you assemble
the beads that call to you; this may be one factor that affects your decisions
on how many of which bead or charm to get. Many pagan traditions and most
pagan divinities have their own symbolism, and if you work in a specific tradition or find yourself called to invoke a particular god or goddess, this can be
an important resource. Another valid approach is simply to ask yourself what
colors and numbers symbolize the things you want your rosary to express.
The following notes, in other words, should not be taken as rules telling you
how to design your rosary. Instead, they are meant as sources of inspiration to
spark your own imagination, intuition, and understanding.

Color

Few pagan rosaries use only one color, and you can combine colors in
many different ways to symbolize whatever you feel your rosary should express.
For example, red, orange, and yellow can be used to represent fire, energy,
and zest for life. Combine the same colors with a tawny brown and you have

a rosary colored like autumn leaves, suitable for any deity associated with harvest or the autumn half of the year. Shades of green make a good combination for vegetation, plants, life energy, or earth energy, while shades of green along with brown and gold symbolize the wild woodlands and the summer. For a water or ocean rosary, you can use different shades of blue, especially with seed pearls or pearlescent white beads. Mix in some green and you have a visual image of all the waters of the world; add brown and golden yellow and you have a rosary of the planet Earth.

Following are some traditional color symbolisms. You can augment these with your color correspondences.

Red: Energy and vitality. As an image of blood, red stands for menstruation and the onset of menstruation at menarche, but it can also stand for hunting, sacrifice, and other ways of shedding blood. It corresponds to fire and the south; its astrological planet is Mars.

Orange: The harvest and turning leaves; fulfillment and abundance. In some traditions, orange stands for the presence of spirit in matter. Its astrological planet is the Sun.

Yellow: The life of the mind; creative insight and new beginnings. Yellow corresponds to spring and the east; its astrological planet is Mercury.

Green: Nature and the natural world; fertility, especially in relation to plants and trees; sexuality and youth. Green corresponds to Earth and the north; its astrological planet is Venus.

Blue: The ocean and all water; wisdom and peace. Blue corresponds to water and the west; its astrological planet is Jupiter.

Violet: Spirituality and the unseen; the realm of subtle and transformative powers that shape our lives. Violet's astrological planet is the Moon.

Black: Solitude, impersonality, and material strength. For far too long, Western culture has seen black as the villain of the color wheel. Black's astrological planet is Saturn.

Brown: Earth, stability, groundedness, and old age. Brown's astrological planet is the Earth.

White: Purity, clarity, and potential that has not yet been manifested. White's astrological symbol is the Zodiac, the circle of stars against which the planets move.

Symbolic Shapes

Any good bead store can provide you with a selection of charms and pendants to add to your rosaries. You may also find beads shaped or painted to represent some of the following symbols. Remember that the meanings of symbols given below are suggestions, not hard and fast rules. Use them to inspire your own sense of symbolic meaning.

Acorns: The life force; especially appropriate for rosaries for forest deities and Druid spiritual practices.

Ankhs: The ancient Egyptian hieroglyph for life; symbolic representation of the female reproductive organs with close links to the goddess Isis.

Bears: Strength and wild energy; in Druid lore, they represent the northern quarter of the world and the element of earth. The bear is one of the most powerful and honored totem animals in many Native American cultures.

Bees: Messengers of the Otherworld; symbol of wisdom.

Birds: The element of air; the soul. Birds are sacred to deities like the Welsh bird goddess Branwen.

Boars: Strength and courage; sacred to the Norse god Frey.

Buffalo or bison: Among the most honored Native American totem animals. Buffalo have potent links to the North American land and, on this continent, should always be considered in rosaries meant to work with earth energies.

Bulls: Strength and fertility; sacred to many thunder gods, including the Celtic god Taranis and the Hindu god Indra.

Butterflies: The soul; transformation.

Cats: Sacred to the Norse goddess Freya and the Egyptian goddess Bastet. Cats symbolize fertility and pleasure. In magical symbolism, the cat represents the Moon.

Celtic knots: The interdependence of all things. These knots also have a place in rosaries dedicated to Celtic deities.

Circles: Wholeness, community, and the universe. Every rosary that has a closed loop of beads, of course, already includes a circle!

Cows: Lunar energies and the powers of fertility. Cows are sacred to many deities, including the Greek goddess Hera.

Dogs: Lunar energies; protection and guardianship. Dogs are sacred to Hermes, the Greek god of communication, trade, and trickery. In magical symbolism, they represent the planet Mercury.

Dolphins: Powers and magic of the sea. Dolphins are sacred to sea deities, and also to the Greek god Dionysus.

Doves: Sacred to the Greek goddess Aphrodite. In magical symbolism, doves represent the planet Venus.

Dragonflies: Transformation and wisdom.

Eagles: The element of air in many magical traditions; transformation and clear sight. Eagles are sacred to the Greek god Zeus; in magical symbolism, they represent the planet Jupiter.

Equal-armed crosses: The four elements and four directions of the magical universe.

Eye of Horus: Used by the ancient Egyptians as a symbol of protection against evil. It represents Horus, the warrior god who vanquishes the powers of night.

Feathers: The element of air; bird deities like the Welsh goddess Branwen. In Egyptian tradition, the feather is also a symbol of truth and the goddess Maat, who represents universal truth.

Fish: The element of water and the powers of the sea. Fish shapes may be used in rosaries for sea deities like the Greek god Poseidon.

Flames: The element of fire. Flame shapes may be used in rosaries for all fire deities, like the Hawaiian volcano goddess Pele and the Greek craftsman-god Hephaestus.

Flowers: Meanings vary depending on the type of flower depicted. In general, flowers are emblems of renewal, life, and love, and belong in rosaries for deities of nature, love, and rebirth.

Grape leaves: Sacred to Bacchus and other gods of celebration and intoxication.

Hawks: The eastern quarter of the world and the element of air in the Druid tradition. Hawks are also sacred to the Egyptian god Horus, the avenger of the gods.

Hearts: Love. Hearts belong in any rosary dedicated to love deities or love magic, but they also represent the soul and consciousness and may be used in rosaries for meditation and spiritual development.

Horses: Powerful solar symbols; strength, fertility, and freedom.

Hummingbirds: The presence of divinity in nature.

Ivy leaves: Sacred symbol of Dionysus, the Greek god of transformation and wild magic.

Leaves: Nature and the living Earth; especially suitable pendants in Druid rosaries. Their symbolism varies depending on the plant from which they come, but any leaf can be used in a rosary for a forest deity.

Lions: Masculine solar symbol; the Sun's fierce light and heat; sacred to many sun gods. In magical symbolism, lions represent the Sun. The lioness is the feminine equivalent, and is especially sacred to the fierce Egyptian goddess Sekhmet.

Lotuses: Purity and the movement of the soul toward enlightenment; among the most profound spiritual emblems in Oriental traditions. Lotuses have a place in rosaries for meditation and for all Oriental deities.

Moons: Varies in meaning depending on its phase—waxing (crescent open toward the left), full, or waning (crescent open toward the right). In Wicca and related traditions, the waxing Moon represents the Goddess as maiden, the Full Moon represents the Goddess as mother, and the waning Moon represents the Goddess as crone. Moon shapes may also be used for deities like the Welsh lunar goddess Arianrhod or the Babylonian Moon god Sin.

Mice or rats: The element of earth; messenger from the earth deities. The rat is the sacred animal of Ganesha, the Hindu god of wealth.

Oak leaves: Among the major holy symbols of the Druid tradition, they are also sacred to many thunder gods, including the Greek god Zeus and the Gaulish god Taranis, and to forest deities of all kinds.

Pentagrams or pentacles: The four elements in balance with the fifth element of spirit. These shapes are emblems of the religion of Wicca, and have been adopted by most branches of the Pagan community as a symbol of earth spirituality.

Pigs: The element of Earth; sacred to many deities of death and transformation. In modern Wiccan symbolism, pigs represent the Goddess in her crone aspect.

Rainbows: Hope and possibility. Rainbows have been adopted in recent decades as an emblem of tolerance and the celebration of diversity.

Roses: Love of all kinds, from the most passionate and sensual dimensions of physical love to the heights of spiritual devotion. Use them in rosaries for love deities, and in any rosary you intend to use for devotional prayer.

Ravens: Wisdom and the passage from life through death to new life. Popular symbols in the modern Pagan community, they are also sacred to the Norse god Odin and the Irish warrior goddesses Badb, Macha, and the Morrigan.

Salmon: Wisdom; in Druid tradition, the western quarter of the world and the element of water.

Scarabs: The Sun in ancient Egyptian tradition; a principal holy symbol for worshippers of the Egyptian gods.

Shells: The sea and the element of water. Shells belong in rosaries intended for water magic, or consecrated to gods and goddesses of the sea.

Snakes: Wisdom and immortality; the energies of the living Earth. Snakes are sacred to many deities, including the Vodoun loa Damballah.

Spirals: Profound emblems of creation and cyclic change. Spirals can be used in rosaries for the deities of creation, birth, and death.

Stags: A complex symbol. In Druid tradition, stags represent the southern quarter of the world and the element of fire; in Wiccan tradition, they symbolize the Horned God and the masculine energies of the cosmos. Stags are also sacred to the Celtic fertility god Cernunnos and the Japanese war god Hachiman.

Stars: Inspiration; emblems of sky deities like the Egyptian star goddess Nut. Four stars placed at equal intervals around a rosary can stand for the four Royal Stars of magical tradition, the guardians of the four Watchtowers.

Suns: Creative power and enlightenment; central symbol in many magical traditions. Suns may also be used in rosaries for sun deities such as the Celtic sun god Belenos and the Japanese sun goddess Amaterasu.

Waves: The sea and the element of water; birth and creation.

Wolves: Wilderness and the powers of nature. Among the most popular of Pagan symbols nowadays; also sacred to the Norse god Odin, the All-father, and many warrior gods and goddesses. In magical symbolism, wolves represent the planet Mars.

Stones

An entire branch of natural magic—the art of using the magical powers in material substances—deals with the subtle powers and influences of different varieties of stone. Many of the most popular stones found in bead stores today have traditional magical uses, and these can certainly be included in a rosary. Following are some traditional correspondences and meanings of ritual stones.

Agate: Courage and confidence; the power to banish hostile spirits and turn aside magical attack. In magical symbolism, agate represents the planet Mercury.

Amber: Strong protective powers against hostile magic; calms the nerves and brings mental clarity. Amber is the fossilized resin of prehistoric pine trees. In magical symbolism, it represents the Sun and may be used in rosaries for all solar deities.

Amethyst: Legendary in ancient times for its power to prevent intoxication; its name comes from a Greek word meaning "not drunk"! Amethyst also helps open the subtle senses and makes visionary states easier to attain. In magical symbolism, it represents the planet Jupiter.

Bloodstone: The life force; suitable for rosaries dedicated to warrior deities. Bloodstone was also used for weather magic to summon thunder and lightning, and therefore may be used for thunder gods as well. In magical symbolism, it represents the planet Mars.

Carnelian: Banishes shyness, forgetfulness, and anger; helps bring clear thought. Opaque carnelian beads should be added to any rosary containing onyx to counteract the latter's difficult qualities.

Citrine: The element of air; brings mental clarity and insight.

Garnet: The element of fire; gives persistence and a strong will. An oath sworn on a garnet is impossible to break. Garnet also helps the wearer remember dreams and banishes nightmares, so it is an excellent stone for dream work.

Jade: The most important magical stone in Oriental lore. Traditionally, it was said to grant victory in any struggle, and can be used in magical combat to reflect hostile spells back on their sender. Jade blesses gardens and has a place in weather magic to bring rain. In magical lore, it represents the element of earth.

Jadeite: One of the two minerals that forms jade; has the same properties.

Jasper: Powerful protective stone; banishes hostile spirits and negative magic. Red jasper is suitable for rosaries dedicated to warrior gods and other divine protectors. Green jasper is traditionally used for vegetation magic, and was much used in ancient times for weather magic to bring rain.

Jet: Used for many centuries to banish every kind of harmful influence, whether physical or spiritual. Jet is also appropriate for rosaries for underworld deities and for work with ancestors.

Lapis lazuli: Banishes depression; a stone of friendship that has the most power when given to you by a friend. Lapis amplifies constructive emotions and aids in spiritual development. In magical symbolism, it represents the planet Jupiter.

Moonstone: The Moon. Useful in rosaries for all Moon deities or for magical work with lunar energies, moonstone also calms the mind and has the ability to deepen meditative states. It was traditionally used for fertility and agricultural magic. In magical symbolism, of course, it represents the Moon.

Moss agate: Traditionally used in garden magic; its wearer will always have a green thumb. Moss agate should be considered for rosaries for earth magic of all kinds, for fertility, and for deities of agriculture.

Nephrite: One of two minerals that forms jade; has the same properties.

Ocean fossils: Excellent additions to rosaries for sea deities or whenever the magical energies of water are appropriate.

Onyx: Traditionally an unlucky stone because it breaks emotional relationships; has great value in rosaries meant to bring detachment and releasing the past. Combine onyx in a rosary with carnelian to balance its potentially negative energies. In magical symbolism, it represents the planet Saturn.

Pearl: Feminine energies; the Moon and the sea. Pearls are especially appropriate for all ocean goddesses, but may be used in a rosary for any goddess. In magical symbolism, they represent the energies of water.

Quartz crystal: The Moon. Quartz crystal mirrors and amplifies any energy it encounters, just as the Moon reflects the light of the Sun. It can be used in any rosary.

River stone: Good choice when a rosary is intended for magical work with the element of water; it also belongs in rosaries for river deities.

Rose quartz: Attuned to the planet Venus; has the power to attract love. Rose quartz may be used in rosaries for love deities.

Tourmaline: Brings positive emotional states. Green, blue, and watermelon tourmaline are good for general improvement of the emotional life;

pink tourmaline increases the ability to love; black tourmaline is protective and banishes negative emotional states.

Turquoise: Protects against injury, especially falls; relieves tension and stress; brings affection and true friendship. In magical symbolism, turquoise represents the Moon.

Numbers

Symbolic numbers give you another way of weaving meanings into your rosaries. Pagans nowadays use several different systems of number symbolism, providing even more options. Here, we give systems from three different cultures: the Western magical traditions, the ancient Greek pagan tradition, and the bardic numbers from modern Druid spirituality. The Greek system goes from one to ten, the other two from one to thirteen. You can use any of them, or choose any other way of using numbers that makes sense to you.

One: In the Western magical tradition, unity and the transcendent source of all things. In Greek paganism, the gods Zeus and Apollo; form, limit, and definition. In the bardic numbers of modern Druidry, the unity of all things.

Two: In Western magical tradition, a masculine number of creative force and outpouring energy corresponding to the Zodiac. In Greek pagan tradition, the goddess Demeter, the god Eros, and the Muse Erato, patroness of love poetry; concepts of substance, infinity and freedom. In the bardic numbers, polarity and the harmony of spirit and matter.

Three: In magic, a feminine number of creative form, limitation, and receptivity corresponding to the planet Saturn. In Greek pagan tradition, the goddess Hecate and the Muse Polyhymnia, patroness of rhetoric; prudence, wisdom, and harmony. In the bardic numbers, completion and perfection.

Four: In magic, a masculine number of expansion and beneficence corresponding to the planet Jupiter. In Greek paganism, the hero Heracles, who became a god through his labors for good on earth, as well as the Muse Melpomene, patroness of tragedy; completion and perfection. In the bardic numbers, manifestation.

Five: In magic, a feminine number of change and unification corresponding to the planet Mars; also the individual human being. In Greek paganism, the goddess Aphrodite and the Muse Calliope, patroness of poetry; justice, balance, and sexuality. In the bardic numbers, self-control and clarity.

Six: In magic, a balanced number of harmony, beauty, and reconciliation corresponding to the Sun; the universe. In Greek paganism, the sea-goddess Amphitrite, the spouse of Poseidon, and the Muse Thalia, patroness of comedy; reconciliation, peace, and health. In the bardic numbers, time and patience.

Seven: In magic, a feminine number of victory, love and sexuality corresponding to the planet Venus. In Greek paganism, Athena, the virgin goddess of wisdom, and the Muse Clio, patroness of history; destiny and the power of the gods. In the bardic numbers, the Moon as the symbol of transformation and magic.

Eight: In magic, a masculine number of clarity, intellect, and analysis corresponding to the planet Mercury. In Greek paganism, the goddess Rhea and the Muse Euterpe; wholeness and safety. In the bardic numbers, purification and cyclic change.

Nine: In magic, a balanced number of foundation, imagination, and transformation corresponding to the Moon. In Greek paganism, the goddesses Hera and Persephone and the Muse Terpsichore, patroness of dance; concord and limitation. In the bardic numbers, knowledge.

Spacers or Not?

When working on your rosary design, one thing to consider is whether or not to use spacers. You can include them for aesthetic reasons, or for functional reasons. But what function do spacers serve in a rosary, anyway? The answer is simple: they do two things. The first is to separate the primary beads slightly so that your fingers can more readily track the shift from one bead to the next. If you're using the rosary to count something, or to delineate steps in a meditation or ritual, this helps you keep an accurate sense of where you are. For someone with a diminished sense of touch, it also helps them notice the movement of the beads through their fingers.

The second function relates to the lifespan of the rosary. Normally, if you string a rosary without giving the primary beads "wiggle room," the strain that this places on the stringing material causes it to snap eventually. Stringing the rosary more loosely allows the beads to shift without stressing the stringing material, but it also allows the beads to rub against the stringing material and eventually wear through it. Spacer beads minimize the degree to which the primary beads shift when handled, thus also minimizing the degree to which they rub on and wear out the stringing material. Spacers also provide the "wiggle room" necessary to keep the stringing material from being too taut, without exposing any of the stringing material between beads. Clare has found that because of these factors, using spacer beads increases the lifespan of a rosary and allows greater leeway in the choice of stringing materials when your selection (or budget) is limited.

Ten: In magic, a balanced number of manifestation and material strength corresponding to the Earth. In Greek paganism, the god Pan and the Muse Urania, patroness of astronomy and astrology; fate, eternity, and necessity. In the bardic numbers, prophecy.

Eleven: In magic, a feminine number of challenge, transformation, and power; the relationship between the individual human being and the universe. In the bardic numbers, fertility, maternity, and creativity.

Twelve: In magic, a masculine number of wholeness, cyclic change, and balance; the wheel of the zodiac as the framework of existence. In the bardic numbers, divine purpose and the influence of destiny.

Thirteen: In magic, a balanced number representing unity and love; closes the cycle of magical numbers, returning to unity. In the bardic numbers, rebirth and transmigration.

How do you use these numbers in making a rosary? Any way you want. If you want to use the number five, for example, you can string the beads of your rosary in groups of five, with a spacer, a charm, or a different bead separating the groups. You can also have five charms in the rosary, or five groups of beads. Or you can combine numbers by adding or multiplying them. The Druid rosary of the Four Elements described in chapter 5 (see page 104), for example, uses four octaves, or groups of eight beads, to represent the eight festivals of the Druid year in each of the four elements. If you decide to use number symbolism in your rosary, you can weave numbers together in any way that appeals to you.

Modifying a Design

What if you see a design you like, but it has some details you find unsatisfying? Go ahead and play with it; change what you don't like and see what you can come up with to make the design work better for you.

First, clarify in your own mind what it is about the existing design that you don't like. This may be obvious—the strand in the photo has amethyst beads in it and you hate amethyst, or it has a pendant and you want to make your rosary without a pendant. Or the issues may be more complex than that. You may find several things you want to change—perhaps a material you don't like and one or more design elements. For instance, in the Triple Goddess rosary (see page 122), you may find it more satisfying to use nine spacer beads instead of three between each set of nine main beads, or you may want to use thirteen main beads for each set and add a pendant of nine main beads between the circlet and the spiral charm. Sit down with the original design, a sheet of paper, and a pencil. Look at the original design in both its broad outlines and its fine details; make notes on everything you like and dislike about it. If you feel inspired, sketch the design with some of your own ideas included, or use any of the ideas given above to stimulate your own creative process. Give your deep mind a chance to work. Then take what you've come up with and see where it leads you.

What if you don't like the pendant on the Four Elements rosary (see page 105)? It's fairly easy to leave a pendant out, even if that changes the symbolism of the rosary slightly. In this example, you can simply use a single spirit bead to close the rosary and bring it full circle, or you can omit both spirit bead and ivy leaf, ending the earth octad with the two spacer beads that would have preceded the ivy leaf. The next item would then be the air feather, wrapping around the year to begin again with winter's transition into spring.

On the other hand, what if you want to add a pendant to the Three Realms rosary (see page 111)? That's a bit more complicated than simply removing the pendant from the Four Elements rosary and closing it up between earth and air. Why? Balance and symmetry. The Four Elements rosary is based on a fourfold pattern accented by five charms. It's the fifth charm that keeps the rosary symmetrical with the presence of the pendant. If you want to add a pendant to the Three Realms rosary, which uses three charms, you have two choices: either add a fourth charm, which preserves the symmetry but changes the symbolism somewhat, or create a design that is balanced, but not symmetrical.

For example, Clare created a rosary in which she substituted beads for charms, added a fourth bead, and then added a pendant. She used the four beads to symbolize the four cities of Gorias, Falias, Finias, and Murias, the places from which the Tuatha de Danaan, the high faerie of ancient Ireland, brought their four treasures. The pendant then incorporated beads with related symbolism. If you want to add a pendant to your Three Realms rosary but not add a fourth charm, try some sample sketches or bead layouts to get a clear sense of what your options are. Then do some brainstorming to decide where you want to add the pendant and what you want to include in it.

Miniaturizing a Design

What if you like a design—your own or someone else's—very much, but for some reason you need a smaller version of it, perhaps something you can tuck into a pocket? There are several simple ways to go about this.

- Use smaller beads for either your primary beads or your spacers, or both; this can reduce the size of a rosary by more than you may expect.

- Use fewer beads; where the design calls for three beads each of three colors to make a set of nine, use one bead of each color to make a set of three. This is a particularly useful technique when you need to downsize a design to make a jewelry version of it. (See chapter 8 for more details on converting a design into a wearable rosary.)

- Use fewer sets; if the design calls for eight sets of four beads each, use four sets of four beads.

- Use more spacers and fewer primary beads; this makes a rosary that can be folded or coiled into a smaller space. It also makes for a less expensive rosary, since spacer beads are usually much cheaper than primary beads.

- Use only seed beads in two sizes—6/o for your primary beads and 11/o or 12/o for your spacers.

Several pocket-sized rosaries are shown in Figure 2-6. All three of the Wiccan rosaries in Figure 2-7 can readily be tucked into a pocket, as can the Three Realms rosary in Figure 2-1 or Grandma-san's memorial rosary in Figure 1-1. As these examples demonstrate, bigger is not necessarily better and small can be quite beautiful!

Figure 2-6.
All of these rosaries
are small enough to
fit in your pocket.

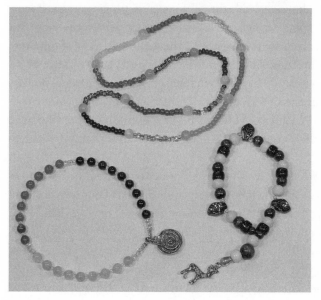

Figure 2-7.
These Wiccan
rosaries are also
pocket-sized.

Designing on a Budget

Budget an issue? That's true for a lot of people these days. But rosaries can be designed using inexpensive, yet good-quality, beads and charms; you can do a lot more than you may expect for between $6 and $20. Beading on a budget is possible, especially if you have a good bead store within reach. The keys to designing a beautiful, inexpensive rosary are simple: use quality beads made of glass, wood, or bone costing no more than 15 cents apiece, and use a minimum number of charms and/or more expensive beads.

Your best bet is to buy your primary beads in a store that sells them by the bead rather than by the package or strand, so you can limit the quantity you have to purchase. A strand of beads can mean a lower per-bead cost, but it also means a higher up-front price unless the strand contains almost exactly the number of beads you need. It also helps to shop at a store that sells stringing materials by the yard, so you can buy a single yard instead of a package; again, this means a lower up-front cost. Not all stringing materials are sold by the yard, however; silk thread for pearl-stringing, for instance, normally is not. Yet some stringing materials are inexpensive enough that you can easily afford an entire package; as of this writing, a spool of Superlon the size of a sewing machine bobbin, for example, costs around $1.50 or so. When in doubt, don't hesitate to price your chosen stringing material both by the package and by the yard to find out which is more economical for your needs. Most bead store clerks are quite used to waiting on people who need to figure the cost of their project, and will be friendly about helping you with the prices.

Let's look at a few specific rosaries, using prices current in the autumn of 2006. (Check prices at your own bead store and calculate your own costs, of course, before trying to design an inexpensive rosary.) The glass-bead Four Elements rosary in Figure 2-8 cost approximately $6.50 in beads, plus spacers and stringing material. If you have to buy a bottle of seed beads and a yard of waxed linen thread, that adds about $3, for a total cost of $9 to $10 before sales tax (if any). The glass-bead Three Realms rosary in the same figure cost

Figure 2-8. Two inexpensive but beautiful glass-bead rosaries.

just under $4 for beads, plus stringing material and seed-bead spacers, so can be made for approximately $7 if you have to purchase everything instead of using seed beads and stringing material left over from a previous project. In both cases, Clare already had suitable seed beads and stringing materials, so her immediate out-of-pocket cost on the two together was just under $10.50. A wood-bead Three Realms rosary (see page 111) can be made inexpensively by buying a packet of 10mm or 12mm wood beads with at least nine each of three colors of bead in the packet and omitting spacers from the design. These beads retail for about $3 per packet; add 25 to 50 cents for a yard of mouse-tail or bug-tail cord or waxed linen thread. Your total cost for such a rosary is therefore approximately $3.50. If you have a source where you can buy wood beads loose, by the bead, you can find these beads for 5 cents to 8 cents apiece, which drops your price to between $1.75 and $2.75. Similar changes can be made for the Triple Goddess rosary illustrated in Figure 6-2 (see page 122); glass beads equivalent in size and quality to the stone beads used in the sample can be purchased for 8 to 10 cents per bead, with a cost for the twenty-seven primary beads of $2.16 to $2.70. The spacers cost $2.00 per bottle; tiger-tail is 50 cents a yard; six crimp beads were 2 cents each. The pendant cost $1.25. Thus you can make a similar rosary of glass beads for between $6.03 and $6.57.

Another budget-saving option is to haunt the Goodwill, the Salvation Army, church bazaars, yard sales, flea markets, and other sources of cheap second-hand jewelry. Many times, these places have old bead necklaces on sale for anywhere from 25 cents to $2. If you find a necklace with beads you just love, you can turn it into a rosary by simply restringing it. You would be wise to clean the beads first, however, to remove the previous owner's energy. For beads that will tolerate water, just wash them in cold running water and let them dry on a paper towel set in the sunlight. For beads that dislike water (for example wooden beads), immerse them in a bowl of dry kosher salt for twenty-four hours, then wipe them with a clean cloth and expose them to sunlight. If you're not sure whether the beads can handle water, choose one you won't mind losing and test it. The results will tell you which method to use. Either way, if you can handle smoke, you can finish up by passing the beads through smoke from a smudge stick or a stick of purifying incense (such as frankincense).

In other words, yes, you can make your own rosary for an affordable price, even if money is tight. Go window-shopping with a sharp eye for both quality and price, and you'll be surprised at the bargains you can find.

3

Choosing Your Materials

BEADS ARE AVAILABLE in a wide range of materials, colors, textures, shapes, and sizes. Stringing materials and "findings" (the jewelry components that hold things together) also vary widely, and include many items that are great for making rosaries. Here are some of the choices available to you.

Beads

Beads come in a fantastic range of shapes. Cubes, rounds, bicones, barrels, chicklets, donuts, hairpipes, rondelles, drops, chips, nuggets, and ovals are common and can usually be found in a choice of several different materials. Plenty of special shapes are available as well. Pressed glass beads may be shaped like hearts, flowers, leaves, and butterflies; horn and bone beads can be found in hourglass, pierced, and intricately carved shapes; shell beads often take spiral or curved forms, while freshwater pearl beads come in rice-grain

Figure 3-1.
A rosary made of glass, metal, bone, horn, stone, and ceramic beads. The spacer beads are metallic colored iris beads.

and potato shapes, and mother-of-pearl is found in long narrow "icicles" and flat thin rounds among others. Many glass beads are embossed or stamped with overlaying designs of stars, moons, faces, fans, cats, and flowers. Lamp-work beads take interesting and unusual forms, and may have little knots or swirls of glass on the surface to provide a pebbled texture. Metal beads may be pierced, openwork, or cast to resemble basketwork or weaving. Ceramic beads are so varied that you can probably find one in almost any shape you can imagine.

Bead Materials

Bone and horn beads come in many interesting colors and textures. Many of them are carved, pierced, and dyed in unusual patterns. These beads are often quite inexpensive, and can sometimes be bought by the strand—a money saver if you will need more than ten to fifteen of the same type.

Ceramic beads are a versatile choice, available in many sizes, shapes, colors, and patterns. Their only disadvantage is that some of them can be fragile. Select beads with relatively thick walls, and check the threading hole for signs of cracking inside. Such cracks, which occur during firing, weaken the bead and can cause it to split suddenly. Glazed porcelain beads are much less likely to be cracked than are rougher clay beads.

Cultured pearls and freshwater pearl beads are available in many shapes and colors. Their luster and sheen are pleasing to the eye, and they work wonderfully well in rosaries relating to water or to sea deities. They often have very small stringing holes, however, so check to make sure your thread will fit, and don't plan on using these in a pendant or another design requiring

Figure 3-2.
A rosary made with stone, metal, metallized plastic, imitation cloisonné, fire-polished, and silver-lined glass beads.

the thread to run through the bead twice unless you are certain that the holes are big enough.

Glass beads are the real workhorses of the rosary beader. They range from inexpensive imported beads to expensive but gorgeous art-beads. They come in a wide range of sizes, shapes, and colors, and you can buy many of them by the strand. Furthermore, it's fairly easy to find good-quality glass beads. Clare relies on glass beads for affordable, light, and portable rosaries. Portable? Yes; if you're going to travel with your rosary, wood or glass beads, which are light weight and fit into a fairly small space, travel well. They also don't set off airport security alarms, and security personnel tend to assume they are items of jewelry. Speaking of jewelry, you can make an astonishing array of wearable rosaries with glass beads for as little as $5 to $6 per rosary (2006 prices). On the other end of the price spectrum, handmade lampwork or dichroic glass beads are unique pieces of art that can add special beauty to a strand of prayer beads. If you enjoy meditating on a candle flame, a lampwork bead with metal foil in its core reflects the light in a way reminiscent of a dancing candle flame. You may consider using such beads in a meditation strand.

Metal beads are available in a tremendous range of sizes, shapes, and textures. You can buy anything from jeweler's-quality gold and silver beads (probably your most expensive option for rosary-making) down to pot-metal *heishi*. Metal beads are frequently decorated with patterns, or are made to resemble other materials such as basketwork. Interesting to the eye and hand, these beads can be found in forms that will symbolize nearly anything you can imagine. You can also find metalized beads, which have a layer of metal over a plastic base. These beads are inexpensive and pretty, but make sure they're good quality before you buy; cheap ones can and do break down, with the metal layer flaking, rubbing off, or changing color.

Most of the moderately priced metal beads are made of pewter. The better manufacturers certify their pewter as lead-free. If you're concerned about the lead content of metal beads you think may be pewter, particularly for a child's rosary, check with your supplier to see if the beads are from a lead-free source. In the higher price range, beads of vermeil, Hill Tribe silver, sterling silver, and 14-karat gold are available in many beautiful shapes. Hill Tribe silver in

Figure 3-3. A rosary to honor multiple deities, showing a variety
of inexpensive but pretty glass beads.

particular often uses nature themes, taking shapes and patterns from plants, animals, birds, and insects. These are beautiful in a rosary. Do be careful with Hill Tribe silver rounds or tubes, however. They are hammered out of relatively soft silver sheets and can be crushed if placed in a position where they'll take the weight of other beads. A good supplier can advise you about whether a Hill Tribe bead they sell can bear weight or not.

Mother-of-pearl beads are beautiful, with a sheen and luster that really catches the eye. You can find them in a range of sizes and shapes, in dyed as well as natural colors, and they are usually reasonably priced as well. They do tend to flake and chip along cut edges, so the thin flat shapes aren't the best choice for rosaries; but the smoothly cut and shaped beads, especially the rounds and rice beads, are wonderful. Watch for narrow stringing holes.

Resin beads look like glass beads with a frosted matte finish. They are a good choice when you want an unusual texture. They are available in a range of soft colors that are popular with children and work well to symbolize spring. Their finish also resembles beach glass, making them a nice addition to a sea rosary.

Shell beads have one problem as rosary components: they can be fragile. The thinner shell beads tend to crack or chip easily, especially when combined with beads that are heavy or hard, like stone or metal beads. However, shell beads make good rosary strands for water, or for deities such as Neptune or Manannan. If you want to use beads made of small whole shells, your best bet is to use them alone. If you want to combine them with something else, use glass seed beads or beads of bone or wood, which are light enough to significantly reduce the risk of breakage. The sturdiest whole-shell beads are small, thick shells that have been drilled or pierced from top to bottom. Cowry shells are the classic example of these. Worked-shell beads resist breakage much better than whole shells do, and offer a wider range of usable choices. Choose worked-shell beads that are made from relatively dense shells; for maximum strength, avoid either curved or hollowed shapes. *Heishi,* rounds and several other sturdy shapes of shell bead are available in different sizes. You can often find them dyed various bright colors as well.

Stone beads are heavy, dense, smooth, and cool to the touch, warming to your hand as you pass them through your fingers. They are available in a wide variety of colors and shapes, and in sizes ranging from 2mm faceted rounds to 24mm tumbled nuggets, with everything in between and a few things beyond. Beaders who are addicted to stone beads, as Clare is, will tell you that nothing matches the silky feel of a well-polished piece of stone. In addition, they're durable and have an unusually high capacity to carry an energetic charge. Stone beads tend to be on the expensive side, but are well worth their price.

Wood beads are an attractive, inexpensive option for many types of rosaries. They come in a range of sizes, and are most often found in round, barrel, oval, or rounded bicone shapes. You can find them in natural browns and creams, and also painted or dyed in various bright colors. Some craft stores carry unfinished wood beads that you can dye, paint, or stain to your own preference. Wood beads are very light for their size, an advantage for those who have limitations of strength or dexterity.

You may have noticed that we haven't mentioned plastic beads. Many plastic beads have certain problems that render them rather unsuitable for rosary making. They tend to develop a slight static charge when handled frequently; their colors are often transient and fade or change within a few months; and they are far too likely to be of poor quality. For these reasons, we don't recommend using plastic beads unless your budget gives you no other options, or unless you find a stash of high-quality beads. If your budget is narrow, try pricing wooden beads or the smaller glass beads, which tend to be fairly inexpensive. Review the detailed discussion of rosary making on a budget in chapter 2 before you shop.

Stringing Materials

Choosing materials on which to string your beads is the next step. What works best for you depends on the beads you've chosen and the type of use and handling your rosary will receive. One stringing material may be perfect for a votive rosary that will rest on an altar and seldom be handled, but a complete disaster for a rosary that will get a lot of daily use and be carried around in a pocket. Another stringing material may be exactly what you need for a jewelry rosary, but have the wrong qualities for a simple circlet of wood beads for a small child. We give general recommendations below, but when reading them, keep in mind that you may need to adjust for your own specific circumstances. Furthermore, changes in the quality of raw materials or finished products are apt to occur. New products of superior quality may be introduced, and existing products may either downgrade in quality or be improved. This section, therefore, is not and cannot be comprehensive. When in doubt, consult with your supplier about the suitability of a stringing material for your purposes.

Beading wire is the most generally useful and durable option for stringing a rosary. It comes in two broad types, tiger-tail and flexible wire. Both are made from the same basic materials—a cable of fine steel wires coated with a thin layer of tough plastic. The major differences between them are flexibility and durability. We'll discuss the basics of both types in the next couple of paragraphs, and go into detail about how to select the size of beading wire you'll need in the Shopping Tips section (see page 65).

Flexible wire, as its name implies, is soft and flexible. Soft-flex and Soft Touch, the best brands of flexible wire, boast accurately that they drape like thread, and can be used to crochet or to make knots. Flexible wire doesn't tend to kink, unlike its heftier cousin, tiger-tail. Therefore, it is perfect for stringing a rosary with a pendant. In spite of being knottable, however, it does require crimp beads to close it, because it doesn't knot tightly enough to remain knotted under the stress of daily handling. It's perfect for pearl or stone beads with narrow stringing holes, since it comes in narrow diameters. Its flexibility also makes it nice to use in any prayer-bead strand that will be worn as a necklace, where drape and hang influence both the appearance and the comfort of the finished piece.

If you want to make a prayer-bead strand that imitates the popular "floating" look in necklaces, with a few carefully chosen beads knotted or crimped into place at intervals on a nearly invisible stringing material, flexible wire is your friend. It's about three times the price of tiger-tail, but the quality is well worth the cost. Many bead stores sell it by the yard, and some sell it in various colors as well. The only drawback to flexible wire is that the very characteristics that give it more flexibility than tiger-tail also give it less strength. If you're planning a strand that uses relatively heavy beads or beads that may have sharp edges, use tiger-tail instead. Likewise, if you're planning to handle your strand frequently, tiger-tail is the better option, because it can handle more wear and tear before it gives out.

Tiger-tail is the industry nickname for the original, heavier form of beading wire that is sold under brand names such as Acculon or Accuflex. Tiger-tail is a good choice for heavy beads, especially those with sharp or rough edges, but it has certain peculiarities you need to be willing to work with or around. As with its more flexible cousin, it has to be closed with crimp beads. If tiger-tail gets a kink or crease in it, that area will be weakened and subject to breakage, so you must be careful handling it to prevent a looped or twisted area from getting pulled into itself and kinking. For this reason, tiger-tail isn't the best choice for stringing rosaries with pendants; the section that forms a loop around a pendant charm can develop a crease, weaken over time, and break, leaving your pendant incomplete. Also, tiger-tail has a certain springiness and rigidity that flexible wire lacks, so unless you are using heavy beads, it can make your finished piece somewhat stiff.

Tiger-tail is a very good choice, however, for necklace rosaries, bracelet/wrist rosaries, and hair-dangle rosaries. All of these styles feature closures such as ring-and-toggle clasps that work well with a crimp-bead closure. Furthermore, the tough resilience of tiger-tail extends the life of "jewelry" rosaries in the face of the everyday wear and tear that they experience. Clare also uses it for large rosaries (those with a total loop length of more than 12") of heavy stone beads, which are usually too hard on anything else.

Bonded nylon upholstery thread, for example that sold under the brand name Mastex, is an acceptable choice for rosaries made of beads with narrow holes. It's strong and wear-resistant. It will fray if rubbed a lot, however, so, as with any type of thread, if you plan to use your rosary daily, it's not the best option.

Elastic is useful for bracelet rosaries, especially those intended for children, but is seldom strong enough to last long. If you want to use something with "give," avoid the various plastic "elastic" cords or threads. These are prone to stretch out of shape quickly unless you are using lightweight plastic beads, and they are also prone to wear out and break very rapidly. Your best bet is to go to a reputable sewing store and buy the thread-covered colored elastic cords such as the better manufacturers of bead bracelets use. Even these, however, may wear out within a couple of months if you wear your rosary every day. Be prepared to check regularly for signs of impending breakage, and to restring the rosary if you see fraying or if the elastic loses its "give."

Some bead stores carry fishing line. Although quite strong, this has the same disadvantage as waxed thread: it frays badly under repeated handling and, for that reason, can break suddenly. Clare's experience with repairing rosaries initially strung on fishing line makes her feel it's not suited for rosaries that will be used regularly. It's an acceptable choice for rosaries that won't be handled much, however.

Mouse-tail and rat-tail (rayon-covered cord available in different colors and thicknesses) are great for beads with larger stringing holes, such as the brightly colored wood beads often sold for children, resin beads, the larger matte-finish glass beads, or some ethnic silver beads. These types of beads make wonderful wrist rosaries, children's rosaries, and rosaries for arthritic people. Just make sure all of your beads have large enough holes for the mouse-tail or rat-tail to pass through. Some stores also carry a very fine grade of this cord, which is called bug-tail. If you can find it, bug-tail works well when the beads' stringing holes are a bit too snug for mouse-tail, or when you need to run the cord through the beads twice.

Narrow but strong nylon threads are acceptable choices for glass, pearl, or stone beads with very small stringing holes. The quality varies a lot from brand to brand, so if you want to use this type of stringing material, check with your supplier to see which brands they advise. Good-quality nylon thread holds up fairly well, as long as you restrict its use to smaller rosaries made of light-weight or small beads. The Thirteen Moons rosary (see page 117), for example, can be strung on it with fairly good results. Nylon thread frays under frequent handling, however, and won't support much weight if you tend to let your rosary hang from your hand. Therefore, if you decide to use it, incorporate spacer beads into your design and string the rosary without too much "wiggle room" for the beads (see the sidebar on page 41).

Silk thread .5 to .6mm thick (also sometimes sold as cord) is an acceptable choice for small rosaries made of stone or glass beads with normal-width apertures, especially when the design includes spacer beads. It must be used with an eye to wear issues, however. Beads with sharp edges will fray and break silk, usually suddenly and without warning. So make sure that, if your beads are sharp-edged or have unevenly drilled stringing holes, you use a material such as tiger-tail or soft-flex instead. Silk also tends to snap when tugged on, so it's best suited to votive or memorial rosaries that will spend most of their time sitting on an altar or hanging on a statue or picture frame rather than being handled frequently.

Waxed cotton thread is commonly available in small spools, often quite inexpensively. This thread is very poorly suited to rosary-making, however, since it does not hold up under repeated handling and breaks easily. Here's a good rule of thumb: If it looks like dental floss, it will break like dental floss. Avoid it!

Waxed cotton cord, on the other hand, is thicker and much stronger than the waxed thread, and makes an excellent choice for stringing rosaries made of beads with larger stringing holes. (Remember to check the size of your beads' stringing holes to make sure the cord will fit!) It's particularly good for rosaries in which you intend to use knots between beads instead of spacers. The knots in cord will normally be visible, unless you can hide them inside a bead with a very large stringing hole, but you can turn this to your advantage by incorporating the knots into your design. If you're not sure whether a stringing material is thread or cord, check to see if it's a single strand (thread) or several threads braided together (cord).

Waxen linen thread, from Ireland, is a good choice for stringing glass beads. The wax allows the beads to shift slightly, as they usually do when you handle a rosary, while minimizing wear. Don't use it with any bead that may have rough areas inside or a sharp edge to the stringing hole, however, because, waxed or not, the thread will still be damaged by these.

Findings

Findings are the jewelry components that hold everything together, from the spring-clasp of your favorite necklace to the French ear-wires from which your earrings dangle. Many jewelry findings are not needed for rosary making. The following may be very useful to you, however, especially in making wearable rosaries.

Catches or clasps (the terms are often used interchangeably) are useful for closing necklace or bracelet rosaries, and for attaching hair-dangle rosaries to a hair clip. Some clasps operate by means of a spring (spring rings or lobster claws), others by simple gravity (ring-and-bar clasps). Several types of clasp are potentially good choices, depending on your needs. Choose one that suits your design, pleases your eye, and is comfortable to use.

Crimp beads are necessary to hold together items strung on beading wire. You pass the beading wire through the crimp beads, through one component of a clasp, and then back through the crimp beads. Then you crush the crimp beads shut around the beading wire, holding it securely. Repeat the process with the other component of the clasp to produce a finished piece. Detailed instructions for using crimp beads are provided in chapter 4 on page 34.

Hook-and-eye clasps are a jeweler's equivalent of the hooks-and-eyes that are used to fasten clothing. They work in the same way. They are not suited for use with light-weight beads, however, as they require tension (exerted by the weight of the beads pulling downward on the clasp) to help keep them closed. They're very good for heavier pieces.

Jump rings are rings of metal wire that are used as one half of certain types of clasp. Think of the ring that hooks into the spring ring of a necklace clasp; this is a jump ring. Jump rings can also be used for other purposes, such as to attach a lobster claw clasp to a hair clip for hair-dangle rosaries. Soldered

Figure 3-4. A bracelet rosary with a ring-and-bar clasp.

Pagan Prayer Beads

jump rings are the only kind that can be used with beading wire, however, because the opening of a regular jump ring will allow the beading wire to slip out of the ring. You can buy soldered jump rings at any bead store.

Lobster claws are a popular type of spring clasp that are shaped—surprise—roughly like a lobster's claw. Part of one side of the clasp opens to accept or release a ring, and springs shut again to hold it. Many people find lobster-claw clasps easier to operate than the more common spring-ring clasp.

Ring-and-bar or ring-and-toggle clasps (also known simply as toggle clasps) have a long, narrow bar as one component and a ring, a hollow square, or a loop as the other. They operate by passing the bar sideways through the ring and then turning it flat to catch across the opening of the ring. As with hook-and-eye clasps, they require tension to keep them shut, so they aren't a good choice for pieces made of small light beads, but they are wonderful for large or heavy beads. Clare uses them frequently for pieces made from stone or larger glass beads. These clasps are easy to operate one-handed, and are a good choice for bracelets and necklaces. They also come in a wide range of sizes, shapes, and decorative motifs. A well-chosen ring-and-toggle clasp can really "make" a piece.

S-hooks are, in effect, a doubled hook-and-eye clasp. The hook is S-shaped, and a ring passes over each end of the S. Again, these clasps require tension, so if you select one of these, make sure your piece will be heavy enough to exert the required downward drag. These clasps also come in a range of decorated versions.

Split rings are a miniature version of the ring that holds your keys. They're basically a short section of very tightly coiled spring. To thread anything onto them (such as a charm), you need to pry one end open the same way you need to pry your key-ring open to accept a new key. The best use for split rings is to match them with an S-hook clasp, especially for a jewelry rosary strung on beading wire. Split rings are inexpensive and strong, and they anchor the beading wire without any possibility of it slipping out of the split.

Spring rings are a common necklace fastening. These are the rings that have a short spring-driven section that you pull back by means of a little projecting nub, opening the ring to accept or release a jump ring. They work very well for pieces made of small or light beads, although some people find them hard to operate. Spring rings are available in many sizes and several different metals, so they are a versatile option for jewelry rosaries.

Tools

You don't need many tools for making prayer beads and rosaries, but a few items are either required or very useful.

Bead boards are a splendid invention. They are boards, usually made of plastic, that have a U-shaped channel around the perimeter and several compartments in the center. The compartments hold loose beads and other materials, and the channel allows you to lay out your beads in order prior to stringing them. Many bead boards have $1/4$ inch measurements marked along the channels, which is an extra help for making wearable rosaries. Bead boards are so well designed to aid the creative process that they are more than worth their very reasonable purchase price. Average cost of a good basic bead board as of autumn 2006 is between $5 and $9.

Bead mats—rectangles of vellux fabric, available in various colors—are useful in the layout process if you don't have or don't want a bead board (or sometimes even if you do). They're also great to use as a surface on which to pour out beads; they protect the beads from damage and absorb much of the kinetic energy that would otherwise send beads bouncing and rolling all over the place. Small dishes are also helpful for holding beads as you work, if you decide not to get a bead board. Any shallow dish, saucer, or small bowl will do.

Glue is important for securing the knots of thread- or cord-strung rosaries. If you make rosaries, a good neutral-pH PVA craft adhesive that dries clear and remains flexible is one of your best friends. These adhesives can be found at craft and art supply stores if your bead store doesn't carry them. Plain old school glue will work in a pinch if you don't have anything better on hand, and so will clear nail polish.

Needles are vital for stringing with thread or silk cord. Your best option is to use wire needles. They are thin and flexible, and will slide through partially blocked stringing holes, bend around obstacles, and make their way into or through places normal stiff beading needles can't go. Even if your chosen stringing material comes with a needle woven in, buy two or three extras. You'll probably need one for finishing the piece, and you'll need to have a spare in case one gets damaged or its eye breaks. Luckily, wire needles are reasonably priced! You should only need to use needles if you're stringing your piece on silk cord or a thin nylon thread such as Superlon, or if you're stringing a piece with a pendant. Other stringing materials we recommend will normally pass through the beads without help.

Pliers are indispensable if you are using beading wire. If you're likely to do much beading to make prayer beads or jewelry, a good pair of chain-nosed pliers is worth its weight in gold. They snug into fairly narrow spaces to crush crimp beads, they grip firmly without doing damage, they open jump rings smoothly, and they generally give you a third hand to hold something when you're juggling several items at once. Chain-nosed pliers run between $5 and $40, depending on quality; a decent pair can be bought for about $10. If you're really sold on beading wire and expect to use it often, you can get a pair of crimping pliers that do nothing else but crush crimp beads. They're wonderful to use, producing a secure and visually attractive closure. If you have already bought chain-nosed pliers, don't worry. They are still great for other tasks. Crimping pliers cost between $14 and $25. A regular pair of small needle-nosed pliers with a box joint will do the job in a pinch. You can use the box joint to crush crimp beads shut. This may put your other beads at risk of being crushed, however, as the box joint is usually too wide for the job. If this is the case, try adding a couple of extra crimps to your strand to put the other beads farther away from danger.

Scissors are the other indispensable tool. Get a pair that is small, reasonably sharp, and can cut beading wire without being damaged. The tougher varieties of cheap folding scissors sold in fabric shops are perfect. Keep them sharp, or replace them regularly!

Storage containers are useful if you decide that making a single rosary won't be the end of your beading career. These can range from plastic baggies to compartmented boxes, depending on your needs and budget.

Tape is very useful if you work much with the rat-tail family of cord, with nylon upholstery thread, or with waxed linen thread. Wrap a short piece of ordinary cellophane or transparent tape tightly around the cut end of the cord or thread before you string beads on it. This prevents the material from fraying, and also makes a stiff section of cord, like the tip of a shoelace, that will slide easily though the beads. The tape is difficult to remove, though, so plan to cut off the taped part of the cord.

Tweezers aren't mandatory, but can be so useful that Clare always keeps a pair handy.

Before You Shop

Take some time to think about your project. If you're making a rosary from a design given in this book, think about what bead colors and materials appeal to you or seem appropriate. Do you want all your beads to be made of one material, or do you want variety? If your rosary contains beads referring to the four elements, do you want to use stone for earth, shell for water, metal for fire, and wood for air? And do you want to stick to the traditional elemental colors of yellow, red, blue, and dark green, or would you rather use blue beads for air, sea-green for water, yellow or orange for fire, and black for earth?

If you're working on a design of your own, see chapter 2 for hints on how to use the early phases of the design process to help your shopping go smoothly. Even if you're the sort of beader who simply goes to the store and looks for what strikes your eye, ready to create a design from what chance brings your way, take a few minutes to focus on your purpose before you set out. This will alert your deep mind that its feedback is needed and will encourage your creativity to flow.

Shopping Tips

As we've seen, there are enough different beads out there to create almost anything. You will find many beads that are likely to be suitable for your purposes, but some will inevitably be better than others. When shopping, keep the following points in mind.

What size bead is comfortable to your hand? Most people like beads in the 10-12mm range, but if you have an unusually large or small hand you may want to size your beads accordingly. Beads smaller than 8mm are more difficult to tell apart by feel, and beads larger than 16mm can be unwieldy to handle. Choose a size range that makes your beads comfortable to hold and to pass through your fingers. Spend a few minutes handling the beads you like. This will tell you if they fit your hand comfortably and feel good to the touch.

While checking the fit of the beads, also check the texture. You want beads that feel pleasant to your fingers. There's no use in buying something that looks pretty but feels sticky, oily, scratchy, or otherwise uncomfortable. Handle the beads you are considering; if they feel nice now, they'll feel nice in the finished product. If they feel wrong now, however, don't expect them to improve. Pretty Indian glass beads that have a slightly sticky feel will still feel sticky later, even if you wash them. They may also leak a residue or leave your fingers smelling like chemicals. A metal bead with an unpleasantly nubbly texture won't smooth out until you've handled it many times. That rough spot on the edge of the tumbled-stone spirit bead will snag your fingers every time you go past it. Something that catches your attention in a bad way will continue to do so, lessening your enjoyment of your rosary, just as something that catches your attention in a good way will enhance your pleasure in your rosary every time you handle it. Let your fingers have the deciding vote over your eyes in this issue!

Apart from size and texture, what materials attract you for the different sections of your rosary? If you've taken our advice about advance planning, you have already put some thought into this, but notice what catches your attention in the store as well. You may find something wonderful that you didn't know existed. Maybe you originally wanted to use shell beads for water in a Four Elements rosary, but decided to use blue glass instead for durability. Then you discover some 12mm mother-of-pearl rounds that wear just as well as glass and have a beautiful subtle glow to them. Think about whether these will give you the watery qualities you originally wanted from shell, while providing greater durability.

Likewise, if you are making a rosary that includes a spirit bead, what draws your eye for that bead? A carved and pierced jade tube? Perhaps a cloisonné bead with butterflies on it? Or is there a perfect flat oval bead of clear rose quartz just crying out to be used? Did you find two large round beads with all of the colors of the rainbow in them? Maybe a couple of vintage Czech glass beads? Even if you are drawn to something that seems to be an odd choice, take a good long look at it and see what ideas come to mind.

You may be surprised to find how a spirit bead can make a rosary. Sometimes, when you find the right spirit beads, everything comes together around them. Don't hesitate to choose your spirit beads first and tailor your other bead choices to fit, or to discard other beads you had previously chosen because they don't go with the spirit beads you've decided you want to use. Spirit beads can tie a rosary together into a visual unity, and often become the focal point for it. Let them be the most important beads in your own rosary if that feels right to you.

Spacer beads need to be chosen with an eye to how well their size matches the size of the beads they will be strung between. Size 6/o seed beads will slide right into the stringing holes of many wooden beads, for example. On the other hand, spacer beads that are almost as large as the beads they are strung between will fail to do their job, which is to separate the main beads so you can more easily feel them as you count or otherwise track your way through the strand. Try to select spacer beads no larger than half the size of the main beads, and preferably no more than one quarter the size.

If your main beads have very large stringing holes, consider using knots between the beads in place of spacer beads. This technique is known as "pearl stringing". (See Figure 3-5 for an example done with rat-tail and wooden

Figure 3-5. A rosary made with wooden beads on a knotted rat-tail cord.

beads.) Mouse-tail, rat-tail, braided cotton cord, leather thong, or other comparatively thick cords serve very well for such a rosary. If you choose to use knots as spacers, be aware that you will need to buy a length of cord at least three times the length you expect your finished piece to be to allow for the knots. This varies a bit from cord to cord, of course; the thicker the cord, the longer a section is needed to make a knot. The length of rat-tail needed is therefore greater than the length of bug-tail needed. No matter how thick your cord, however, your best bet is to buy too much rather than not enough. Clare's rule of thumb is: If you think you need a yard for a simply strung piece, buy three yards for a pearl-strung piece. If you have extra left over, you can always use it for another project—and you'll never have as much left over as you expect.

You can also pearl-string smaller beads using silk cord. However, this type of pearl-stringing is more challenging; doing it properly so that the knots are snug against the beads requires practice. If you're interested in this type of stringing for your prayer beads and you have no experience, see if you can find a how-to video at your public library.

If you plan to use a pendant, what choices do you have for the pendant charm? Look over the selection and see what feels right. The store carries one leafless tree and one tree with the Full Moon shining through its branches; which do you prefer? Did you find a pendant with a *triskele* on one side and a spiral on the other, perfect for your favorite goddess? A Thai penis amulet that Pan or Priapus would love? Is the handblown glass Sun pendant hanging in the display case on the far wall just what you need? Or that big chunky turquoise donut by the cash register? Don't limit yourself to conventional necklace-style pendants with a loop on the upper end. If the item of your choice has a hole through it, you can find a way to work it into your design.

Then there are charms. If you go to a well-stocked store, you're apt to find an embarrassment of riches. How many different types of leaves are available? Flowers? Feathers? If you can get a pinecone in silver, copper, or bronze, which one seems the better fit for the symbolism you are using? Should you want to work with a totem animal, you may be surprised at what you find: bear and wolf of course are available in a wide variety of styles and materials, but dragonfly, butterfly, cat, and others can also be found in many forms.

The selection of charms available on the jewelry market is huge, even if you limit yourself to those made of good-quality materials with decent work-manship. A well complete with movable handle and tiny bucket, a two-sided five-petaled flower, a hand with a spiral in the palm, a leaping trout, a Sun with eight rays emerging from it, a pregnant mother goddess, a hinged clam-shell that opens to reveal a man and woman making love—Clare recently found all these at one shop. And four of them were available in more than one color of metal! As with beads, look through a range of choices before making your selection. Even if you find something that you instinctively know is exactly right, you may find that, two rows down, there's something better still.

When you've found what you want from that treasure trove, one guiding principle is paramount: *buy enough!* When in doubt, buy more than you think you need. Almost as important is a second guiding principle: *Buy now if you can!* Why? Because beads and charms are highly subject to whims of fashion. That lovely strand of carnelian rondelles may not be there next month, because rondelles have become passé and now faceted rounds are all the rage. That silver charm you think will be perfect for Aunt Mabel's crone rosary has been discontinued, and the store only has three left before it's gone forever. The copper hand with a spiral in the palm is from a factory that has fallen months behind on orders; your source may not be able to get more until next year. Unfortunately, none of this information may be available to you when you're in the store. You may, in all innocence, leave thinking you'll go back and buy your item another day, only to find out on your next trip that you're out of luck. Try not to delay buying what you find when you know it's the right thing, because you may get caught this way. Clare's bead box has quite a few odd items in it that she was never been able to find again after her initial purchase. They still come in handy for other projects, but what a pity if you end up having to make do with something second-best because the right thing vanished without warning and you were three beads shy of what you needed! And there's another reason to get one more than you need. If you get your perfect beads home and discover that one of them has a flaw you didn't spot, or if, on laying out your beads, you find you have to change your design, the extra beads you bought may just save you another trip to the store. Both of these have happened to Clare more than once.

An unnoticed flaw in a bead brings us to the quality control front. Remember that not all beads you find will be of good quality and in usable condition, even when you shop with a reputable supplier. It's difficult and labor-intensive for business owners to comprehensively examine every lot of beads, and even the best shop can get duped on occasion. Therefore, get into the habit of checking your beads before you buy them. Here are some specific tips:

- If you use beads of stone, bone, shell, or horn, make sure the holes go all the way through. Often, such beads are carelessly drilled, with narrow holes on one side and wide holes on the other (moonstone and mother-of-pearl are particularly prone to this problem), or with holes that are wide on both ends and narrow in the middle, or with holes that are blocked by debris. Such beads are more difficult to string. Look for relatively wide apertures, and holes that seem to be of even width all the way through. Also, check for holes with broken edges, which are common in certain types of stone bead.

- Flaking around one end of a stone bead marks the exit hole of the drill. A small flaked area is not a problem if you're using tiger-tail for your stringing material; such beads can still both look and feel fine. But a larger broken area looks awkward, feels uncomfortable to the hand, and can indicate the presence of internal cracks that will cause your bead to split later on. Also if you're using a thread or cord instead of a wire-based stringing material, the flaked area will cause wear. Avoid these beads.

- Speaking of cracks, always check stone beads for external or internal fissures and cracks. Be especially careful with beads made of amber, crystal, and other stones that break easily. A crack now equals a split later, which means a repair or restringing job to replace the broken bead—if a replacement of the right size, shape, and color is still available.

- Check glass beads for chips or cracks. These aren't as common in glass beads as they are in some stone beads, but they do occur. The beads that seem to be most prone to them are the pressed glass beads in fancy shapes on the one hand, and Indian glass beads on the other. However, any glass bead can have a crack in it or a chip in any vulnerable location. Take a few seconds to check your beads as you select them, especially around the stringing holes.

- If you use metal beads, especially inexpensive beads that can be very poorly finished, check for rough edges inside the lip. These can snag your stringing material and cause your rosary to break suddenly. If you have a bead reamer or needle files, you can smooth out these rough spots. Sometimes, however, the rough areas are too large or too sharp to be reparable. Clare has even seen beads with metal shavings just inside the edges of the hole, still attached to the bead. Beads with small rough areas can be fine given a little repair work, but anything with more serious problems should be avoided. Smooth beads are the best choice.

• When purchasing colored beads that may be dyed, check to make sure the color doesn't come off with handling! Red or pink coral beads are especially notorious for this, as are red "cinnabar" beads, but others have the problem as well. Dyed beads made of natural materials are always suspect when it comes to color-fastness, so test them before you buy. A little moisture will disclose fastness problems in a split second; often simply rubbing the bead has the same results after a bit longer.

Once you have all of your beads, charms, and pendants selected, you'll need to tie it all together This is where stringing materials, needles, findings, jeweler's pliers, bead boards, and other items come into play. If you're using beading wire, you'll need to keep a couple of points in mind when deciding on which grade (thickness) and strength to select for your rosary.

Tiger-tail and flexible wire both come in several different grades, based on the number and thickness of the strands of metal wire inside the plastic coating. The metal the wire is made from also varies, from brass to stainless steel to sterling silver. All of these factors affect how much weight the material can support, how flexible it will be (in the case of tiger-tail), and how fine a crimp bead you will need to close it. The most common strand counts in beading wire include three, seven, twenty-one, and forty-nine. The total diameter of beading wire, regardless of the number of strands, varies from .010" (available only in Soft Touch brand flexible wire) to .024" (available only in tiger-tail). The test strength of the .010 is usually about five pounds, whereas the test strength of the .024 ranges from about seventeen to about forty pounds depending on the metal. This is the amount of strain the material will take without breaking. As with fishing line, the measure is less a matter of how much weight the material will support on an ongoing basis, and more a matter of how strong a sudden jerk must be to cause the material to snap. Here are some basic rules to follow:

- **The number of strands plus the diameter equals strength.** For heavy beads such as tumbled-stone nuggets, use wire with more strands and greater thickness; for medium-weight glass beads a wire with fewer strands and thinner diameter would be more suitable. *You can't maximize both strength and flexibility; choose one.*

- **Even with flexible wire, the stronger the wire is, the stiffer it is; the more flexible it is, the weaker it is.** If you need it to be really flexible, don't plan on stringing heavy beads with it.

- **The finer the beading wire, the smaller the crimp bead.** If you use .010 beading wire with a large crimp bead, the end will work loose from the crimp under the stress of handling and pop free, scattering your rosary beads far and wide. If you use .024 beading wire with a small crimp bead, you won't be able to complete the assembly until you get a bigger crimp bead, because the small one won't even go onto the beading wire. Most bead stores carry both large crimp beads, which are round and about the size of an 11/0 seed bead, and small crimp beads, which are either round or square and fairly tiny. You can also get crimp tubes, which are about twice the length of a regular crimp bead and fit the larger sizes of beading wire. Some suppliers carry clasps that already have crimp tubes attached to them.

This brings us to another issue in the choice of stringing materials. If you are making a rosary with a pendant, you will run the thread at least twice through the beads that make up the pendant. Therefore, you will want to be very careful to make sure that both the thread and the needle you are using are thin enough to make that repeated journey successfully. If you're using flexible wire, make sure two to four strands of it will fit through the beads and crimps. If you're using some sort of thread, it will need to double back through the eye of the needle, and the whole width of that doubled area plus the needle's eye will have to fit through the bead. Your best bet is to use a wire needle for this purpose; their collapsible eyes reduce the total thickness that must pass through the bead. If you're using silk cord, some brands come with a wire-beading needle woven onto one end of the thread. The woven-in needle allows you to thread the beads without having a second thickness of thread behind the needle's eye.

But What If...

Are you having problems finding the beads or charms you want? Availability of materials can be a pitfall, but so can your own expectations of what you'll find. The most important thing is to look for what draws you, what catches your eye and inspires you. If you go into the store with a fixed idea of The Only Right Thing To Buy, you may end up disappointed, and you may also end up missing something beautiful that would have worked perfectly well. Keep your existing ideas in mind by all means, but also look around and see what else you find.

If, after looking carefully, you find that nothing draws you, try another shop or come back to this one on another day. Find out when the shop expects a new shipment. Ask if they can order items that aren't on display, or if they keep additional stock in the storeroom. Talk to them about letting you look at their supplier catalogs, and whether they are willing to place a special order for you. Don't be afraid to make several trips if need be. But also, don't be afraid to look again at the same items you have already passed over. Clare has often found that something she barely noticed on the first walk through turns out to be just what she was looking for. A bead store is a visually busy place. It's easy to miss something, or not to look closely enough, because there's so much distraction. A second walk through the store, perhaps on another day, may find a treasure you just didn't see the first time.

No bead store within reach of you? Or maybe, for some reason, you can't get to the only one in town? Or worst of all, when you get there, they have absolutely nothing suitable for your needs and there's just no place else to go? Unfortunately, that happens. Shopping on the Web or via a catalog is okay; the real downside for rosary-making purposes is that you can't handle and examine your finds before buying. Even reputable suppliers sometimes have sub-par merchandise or will substitute the next nearest thing without asking you, and not all mail order or web-based stores will let you return things that are wrong.

Even if you can return the merchandise, normally you're still responsible for the cost of shipping both ways. And if (gods forbid, but it happens) your selected beads arrive broken, you have the hassle of getting either the shipper or the seller to take the responsibility and reimburse you for the damage. When you buy in person, you can avoid these problems. However, if you have to shop via mail or the Internet, then your best bet is to find a reputable supplier with a wide selection (see the list in the back of the book for some of these), and take your time with your shopping.

Don't hesitate to call suppliers and ask questions. Most have an 800 number for customer service. We have found that e-mail inquiries are less likely to get answered promptly, so a phone call is definitely best. Clare particularly recommends calling those suppliers who employ beaders in their customer service departments; you get lots of information that way from people who are actually using the company products and who know more about them than just the official catalog description. All of the bead suppliers listed in the back of this book employ knowledgeable, dedicated beaders. Also, make sure you are familiar with the company's policies on merchandise substitutions and returns before you buy. This will help you decide what your best choice is should your merchandise turn out to be broken, defective, or just not what you wanted.

One final piece of advice about shopping for your rosary supplies—relax and have fun! Don't let the many choices and other issues get in the way of the most important part of all, enjoying the process of finding your beads. If you've never beaded before, a remarkable new world is about to open up for you. If you're already a beader, you have a great new project to work on. Let the process be a pleasure to you, and you'll be a lot happier with your results.

Making Your Rosary

BEFORE YOU START laying out and stringing your rosary, make sure you have everything you need! Check against your shopping list and the following materials list to be sure you haven't forgotten anything.

Materials List

To make most rosaries you will need:

- beads, approx 10-12mm, for the main purpose of the rosary (for example, the 36 beads for the elements in the Four Elements rosary)

- special-purpose beads, probably larger than 12mm, that will carry a particular significance in the rosary (for example, a red bead for a Brigid rosary, to represent the fire of her forge)

- spacer beads, probably approximately 4mm or size 6/0 seed beads, to spread out the primary beads, special-purpose beads, and charms or other elements for easier handling

- charms (feathers, flowers, leaves, and an endless et cetera of other possibilities), either for decorative or symbolic purposes

- a pendant charm, if a pendant is part of the design or if you want to add one to a design that does not have one

- stringing material

- if you are using thread, wire needles

- if you are using tiger-tail, crimp beads (a minimum of two for each closure) and findings for closures (such as a toggle-and-bar clasp)

- if you are using wire or tiger-tail, a pair of chain-nosed pliers or equivalent (to bend wire, crush crimp beads, etc.)

- a bead board or mat

- if you plan to use thread or cord, a neutral-PH PVA craft adhesive that will dry clear and remain flexible (this can be found at an arts-and-crafts store if your bead supplier doesn't carry it)

Of course, this list will vary depending on the details of the rosary you are making. It is just intended as a place to start. Personalize it to meet your own needs. Once you have everything together, you're ready to finalize the design and make the rosary!

Laying Out Your Rosary

Anyone who has ever worked in graphic arts or design knows that books, newspaper or magazine pages, and ads all go through a layout process, in which the raw material of text and illustrations are assembled into meaningful patterns. Rosaries are no different. Once you have all of your materials, you need to lay them out in the proper order to make sure the rosary you've envisioned will actually work the way you expect. Even if you've done preliminary sketches—and, in fact, one of the reasons for preliminary sketches, as

Pagan Prayer Beads

the story of the Elder Mother rosary in chapter 2 points out, is to catch design flaws in advance—you may still find some unexpected wrinkles when you have the beads laid out. This is especially true of pendant designs, which have a knack for turning out to be more complicated than they originally looked.

Begin by laying out your beads, charms, and other components on your bead board or mat. Be as certain as possible that you have every bead and charm where it belongs; this is the best time to spot layout errors and correct them. Keep in mind the method you plan to use to string the rosary; this will influence where in the design you start and end your stringing and in what order you want to lay the beads out. Use the detailed stringing instructions given with the Druid and Wiccan rosary designs in chapters 5 and 6 as examples to help you decide how to handle your own design. Generally, you can start and end anywhere you like, depending on where you intend to place the closure—either the knots in the thread or cord, or the item you're going to crimp to the beading wire. Once you have the beads laid out to your satisfaction and you've checked for layout errors, you are ready to finalize the design.

Finalizing Your Design

We talked quite a bit about the design process in chapter 2. Still, the proof of the pudding is in the eating, and the proof of a rosary design is in the making. A design that works on paper or in your head may turn out to have unexpected problems when you lay out the beads in your bead board. Often, these turn out to be simple errors, easily spotted and easily fixed—such as forgetting one of the beads for the pendant. In most cases, such errors turn up when you lay out the beads, and can be fixed at that stage without any problem at all. Some errors, however, are less obvious; these usually show up during stringing. In Clare's experience, about 90 percent of these errors involve the pendant—either the join where the pendant attaches to the rosary, or the pendant design itself. The other 10 percent involve the way the beads you selected work together.

How can you anticipate and avoid these errors? When it comes to problems with the pendant, the simplest way is to test-string the pendant and the beads of the join area on some plain thread before you go on to string the entire rosary. This will reveal in advance any complicating factors that may arise in that area of the rosary.

1. Lay out the beads of the pendant in a compartment of your bead board. Make sure you include the connecting bead.

2. Lay out two of the beads from each side of the join area. (For example, in the Horned God rosary in chapter 6 (see page 124), this would mean laying out all the beads of the pendant, the two 6mm wood beads, and two of the pony beads.)

3. Thread a wire beading needle with ordinary sewing thread. At the end of the thread, tie a spare bead to provide a "stop" that will keep the test-strung beads from sliding off the thread.

4. String the two beads on one side, then the connecting bead and the beads of the pendant, down to the charm or other item that forms the pendant's end.

5. Pass the needle through the stringing hole of the item, creating a loop from which the item can hang.

6. Pass the needle back up through the beads of the pendant and the connecting bead, pulling the loop snug. If you did this correctly, the pendant now hangs from a double thread.

7. String the two beads from the other side of the main circlet of the rosary onto the needle, letting them slide down to rest against the top bead of the pendant. Your test-string is finished.

Hold up the string and look at it. Does it hang well? Do the beads of the pendant work harmoniously together, or are there awkward places where another bead should be inserted? Are any of the beads canted at an angle, or stuck inside the overlarge stringing hole of the next bead, or drilled so far off-center that they look lopsided? Are there any areas of thread showing between pendant beads? When you look at the join, do the two innermost beads of the circlet fit smoothly together above the pendant's top bead, or do they jostle one another, leaving a bare section of thread because they have to compete for space? (This last is caused by the top bead of the pendant being too narrow compared to the combined width of the first beads on either side of the circlet.) Areas of bare thread can be covered by inserting seed beads or other small beads into the design at those points, or by rearranging the beads of the pendant so that each bead fits smoothly with the ones to either side of it.

Beads at an angle, beads stuck inside the adjoining bead, and similar problems can also be fixed by rearranging the pendant beads. A bead drilled far enough off-center to look bad can only be lived with or replaced, unfortunately. Beads that fail to join smoothly above the top of the pendant can be replaced with narrower beads, or you can exchange the top bead on the pendant for one that's wider, or you can use spacer beads to cover enough of the thread to give the primary beads more room.

The most common problem with spacer beads, especially seed beads, occurs when they're small enough to slide right into the stringing hole of the larger beads. This can be quite awkward, requiring a sewing needle to pop the spacer bead back out of the larger bead, then replacing it with a spacer bead or intervening bead that's wider than the hole in the larger bead. One good solution to this is to use a pair of *heishi* or small saucer beads to flank the larger bead, effectively blocking its stringing holes so that the spacer beads won't slip inside.

By the time the test-stringing of the pendant is successfully completed, you've probably solved any design problems. Now is a good time to take a look at the other beads in the rosary to check for exactly the same problems we just discussed—beads that will get stuck in adjacent beads, beads that will slide into the hole of adjacent beads, beads that will hang together at an angle, etc. If you're dubious about any section of the rosary, test-string it in the same way you did the pendant, and hold it up to check. When you've checked everything and it all looks as if it's going to work, you can go on to the actual stringing of the rosary.

Stringing Your Rosary

The specific rosary designs we've given in the following chapters include detailed instructions for stringing those rosaries. What follows are general rules to use when stringing rosaries of your own design.

Rosaries without pendants

These are the easiest rosaries to string, and rarely develop problems unless incompatible beads are placed next to one another or unless you string them too tightly. You can start anywhere you want to in the circle of beads. When you're using thread or cord it's a good plan to begin with a large-holed bead, since when you've finished stringing the rosary you can hide the knot inside the bead, but if you don't have a large-holed bead then just pick a place to start.

Strung on thread or silk cord

1. Lay your beads (and charms, if any) out on your bead board or mat. Put them in the same order you'll want them to be in for the finished piece.

2. Get out your stringing material. Unwind enough of it to complete your project. If you're using a material with a woven-on needle, unwind all of the material. (This will keep you from cutting the needle off of the leftover material when you're finished.)

3. Thread your needle, if the thread or cord doesn't already have one woven on.

4. Tie an extra bead to the end of the thread or cord to act as a "stop" that will prevent your beads from falling right off again. If you're using a silk cord that comes wound on a small piece of card, leave

the last loop of the cord in place on the card; the card will then act as a "stop."

5. Pick which bead you're going to start with, if you haven't already done so.

6. String the first bead. Let it slide all the way down to the end of the stringing material and settle against the "stop."

7. String the next few beads. Slide them down to the first bead.

8. Hold up what you've done so far and check to make sure everything is working the way you want it to. If not, now is the time to make changes!

9. Continue steps 5 and 6 until all of your beads and charms are strung.

10. Examine your rosary one last time to make sure everything is exactly where you want it and looks right. This is your last chance to make any changes, unless you want to restring the whole thing. You may find that you're feeling pretty excited about seeing your rosary take something close to its final shape. Enjoy that excitement, but try not to let it distract you from checking for mistakes.

11. If everything is the way you want it to be, it's time to finish the rosary. Carefully lay it down on your bead board or mat and gently remove the "stop" from the end of the stringing material. Set the "stop" aside.

12. Make sure you have three inches of stringing material left at each end of the strand, to form a knotting allowance. Cut off any excess beyond this allowance.

13. Bring the ends of the rosary together and carefully tie your first knot. Check the knot before you tighten it to make sure you didn't catch any beads in it. If the knot is ok, slowly tighten it until the end beads are touching and no stringing material is visible between the beads in the circlet of the rosary.

14. Tie the second knot, keeping the first knot tight in the process. Your rosary should now be strung tightly enough that there's no visible stringing material between the beads, but if the circlet is rigid then it's too tightly strung and you'll need to loosen the knots a little.

15. When you're sure the rosary is knotted tightly enough but not too tightly, give the second knot a firm tug to settle it. Apply glue to the knot and allow it to dry.

16. If you intend to hide the knot inside one of the beads, do so now, using the instructions from the sidebar Hiding the Knot (see page 91).

17. Finally, snip off the loose ends of the stringing material. Your rosary is finished!

Strung on thicker cord (rat-tail, waxed cotton cord, etc.)

One of the great advantages of stringing rosaries on mouse-tail, bug-tail, or the thicker silk cords, is that you can use knots in the cord as spacers. As mentioned in chapter 3, this solves the problem of how to manage including spacers in a rosary made of beads with large stringing holes. Most threads or silk cords are too fine to work properly in this way, unless you're using smaller beads, but the thicker cords are perfect. Clare has a rosary made of wooden beads strung on rat-tail, with knots for spacers, and the size of the knots relative to the wooden beads is just right. (See Figure 3-5 on page 67.)

To string a rosary on the thicker cords, using knots as spacers, use the following steps:

1. Unwind your length of stringing material and tie a firm knot at one end of it, leaving at least three inches of loose cord end beyond the knot so you'll be able finish the piece later.

2. Tightly wrap a small piece of tape around the other end of your stringing material from the knot you've just tied. You'll be using

the taped end to string the beads on; the stiff taped section will act like a needle in sliding through the beads.

3. String your first bead. Let it come to rest up against the knot you've just tied.

4. Now tie a second knot on the other side of the first bead. Get the knot as close to the bead as you can before you tighten it. If it's too far away, use your fingers or the point of an awl to work it closer before you pull it tight. (This can be difficult with thread, but is fairly easy with the thicker cords.)

5. Repeat steps 3 and 4 until your last bead is strung and is secured on both sides by a knot. Make sure you have at least three inches of stringing material left on the other side of the last knot. If you don't have that much, you may need to remove one bead in order to finish; or, alternately, you can leave your piece open-ended. If you have more than three inches of material left, that's fine.

6. Bring the loose ends of the stringing material together. Tie firmly in whatever type of knot you prefer. Claire likes to use an overhand knot, laying the strands parallel to one another and tying both together in a single knot, but any type of knot except a granny knot (the type of knot most people use to tie their shoelaces) will do. Granny knots slip easily, as any parent of a small child can tell you, and therefore are unsuited to holding your rosary together.

7. Trim any excess stringing material. If you want to put a drop of glue onto the knot for extra security, you may do so. (Note: glue will show on the rat-tail family of cord, although not on waxed cotton cord.)

If you want to string your rosary on a thicker type of cord but don't want to use knots for spacers, follow these instructions:

1. Unwind your stringing material and tie a "stop" at least three inches from one end.

2. Tightly wrap a small piece of tape around the end of cord opposite to the "stop." As described just above, this will be the end you slide through your beads.

3. String your beads on the cord one at a time, letting each one fall down to rest against the one before it. Continue doing this until all of your beads are strung.

4. Carefully remove the "stop," making sure your beads don't begin to slip off of the cord.

5. Make sure you have at least three inches of stringing material at either end of your rosary, to create a knotting allowance.

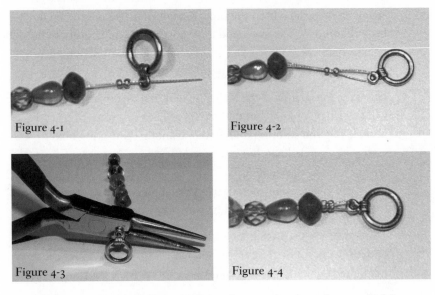

Figure 4-1: The beading wire with beads, crimp beads, and one end of the catch in position, ready to finish. Figure 4-2: Loop the beading wire back through the crimp beads. Figure 4-3: Push the crimp beads together close to the shank of the catch, and crush the crimp beads in the box joint of the pliers. Figure 4-4: The final result, with the beads snugged up against the crushed crimps.

6. Bring the ends of the strand together and finish it with whatever type and number of knots you prefer—always avoiding the granny knot, as discussed above!

7. Trim any loose ends. If you wish, place a drop of glue on the knot(s) for extra security.

Strung on beading wire

The general rules for a rosary strung on beading wire are slightly different. You need two to six crimp beads of the proper size for your beading wire (see the sidebar on page 94 for a discussion of sizing crimp beads and choosing how many crimp beads to use), as well as a pair of pliers to squash the crimp beads shut. You should also keep in mind that you'll need to have the two ends of the beading wire fasten to a clasp of some kind, to the shank (loop) of a charm, or to one another. For example, note in the stringing instructions for the Triple Goddess rosary that the beading wire fastens to the shank of the spiral charm (see page 123). The instructions below include separate sections for the different kinds of closure. Read these before you begin stringing, so you know ahead of time how you're going to need to close your piece. Also refer to Figures 4-1 through 4-4, which illustrate the crimping process, to make sure you are clear on how this works. Once you've made these preparations, you're ready to begin stringing.

1. Unwind a length of beading wire from the spool. *Don't cut the wire yet*; if it's left intact, the spool itself serves as a "stop" to keep your beads from slipping off. (If you're using a precut length of wire rather than a spool, wrap a small piece of tape around one end of the wire, like a flag, to be the "stop.")

2. Thread the number of crimp beads you need for one side of your closure (one to three, depending on your project) onto the beading wire. Let them slide down until they're lying against the spool.

3. Now thread your beads onto the beading wire, in order, until all of them are strung. Make sure you have about three inches of beading wire beyond the beads, for a closure allowance.

4. Next string the crimp beads you need for the other half of your closure.

5. Look below to find the closure instructions which fit your project.

If you are stringing a rosary which closes with a charm, like the Triple Goddess rosary in Figure 6-2 (see page 122):

1. Thread the cut end of the beading wire through the shank of the charm. Now turn the beading wire back around the shank of the charm to form a loop, on which the charm will hang.

2. Thread the end of the wire back through the crimp beads and if possible through several of the preceding beads as well, and pull it fairly snug. Leave enough room in the loop of beading wire for the shank of the charm to move freely.

3. Using pliers, crush the crimp beads firmly around the beading wire. Trim off any exposed end of the beading wire.

4. Then cut off the other end of the beading wire from the spool, leaving two inches or so of beading wire beyond the end of the beads for a closure allowance.

5. Thread the second end of beading wire through the shank of the charm, being careful not to tangle it with the loop of beading wire already there.

6. Repeat steps 2 through 4.

If you are stringing a rosary which closes with a clasp, like the bracelet rosaries in Figure 8-2 (see page 151):

1. Decide which half of the clasp will attach to which end of the rosary.

Where do you put the knot in a thread-strung rosary? Well, that depends on whether the rosary has a pendant or not. If it has a pendant, the knot should be somewhere within a couple of inches of the point on the circlet that is opposite the point where the pendant begins. The reason for this is that the pendant poses the greatest strain on the integrity of the stringing material. If the knot is too close to the pendant, it will be more likely to break than if it is about halfway around the rosary from the pendant. Distance helps even out the weight distribution. On the other hand, if the rosary has no pendant, you can put the knot almost anywhere in the circlet. Always try to avoid placing the knot next to a heavy bead or charm, especially one with a snug stringing hole, because this will also place extra strain on the knot. The best components to place your knot next to are beads with large stringing holes, or failing that, charms with shanks large enough for the knot to slide into. This is because both of these allow you to hide the knot inside them, which lengthens the lifespan of the knot and also makes your rosary look more tidy.

2. Take the clasp half which will attach to the loose end you are presently finishing, and string it on the beading wire.

3. Turn back the beading wire to form a loop attaching the clasp half to the rosary.

4. Thread the end of the beading wire back through the crimp beads and several following beads.

5. Pull it snug, leaving a loop of beading wire just large enough for the shank of the clasp to move freely in.

6. Now crush the crimp beads as described above, being careful not to crush other beads or the clasp.

7. Cut off the other end of the beading wire from the spool, leaving a two inch closure allowance.

8. Thread the remaining crimp beads and the second half of the clasp.

9. Repeat steps 3 through 6.

If you are stringing a hair-dangle rosary:

1. Make sure before you go any further that you have strung it the right way round—the end which is now open should be the end with the charm. Also see Figure 8-3 on page 153, if you want to see in advance what a finished hair-dangle will look like.

2. Close the charm end as described above for a rosary closing with a charm.

3. Cut the loose end of beading wire off of the spool, leaving a $1^1/_2$ inch closure allowance.

4. Now turn the beading wire back through the crimp beads and any following beads until you have a loop of beading wire about $^1/_4$ inch long. This loop will hang from the lobster claw clasp you have already attached to the hair finding.

5. Crush the crimp beads and trim any excess loose end of the beading wire.

If you are stringing a rosary which closes on itself, without a finding or charm:

1. Close the first end by turning back the loose end of the beading wire through the crimp beads and following beads until you have created a loop of wire which is no more than $^1/_4$ inch long—smaller, if you can manage it. This loop is the first half of the closure.

2. Crush the crimp beads.

3. Now cut the beading wire off from the spool, leaving a 2 inch closure allowance.

4. Pass the loose end of the beading wire through the loop you have already made, as though you were passing it through the shank of a charm.

5. Turn it back through the crimp beads and following beads, pulling it snug to create a second tiny loop which is hooked through the first.

6. Crush the crimp beads and trim any excess loose end of beading wire.

If you are an experienced beader and know your way around wire work—the art of making and using shapes of metal wire as part of jewelry—this closure may now be covered up with a wire wrap.

Rosaries with pendants

These are slightly more complex than circlet rosaries, because of the pendant. Still, if you check your beads ahead of time and test-string your pendant, as suggested above, you should have no problems during the actual stringing process. Clare strongly recommends that you use flexible wire to string all pendant rosaries which will be used regularly; it combines flexibility with durability, giving a long working life before the inevitable restringing that all rosaries need in time. However, if your rosary is a votive piece, or otherwise will receive little handling, you could string it on silk cord or waxed linen thread.

For pendant rosaries strung on flexible wire:

1. Assemble your beads, charms, crimp beads, wire, pliers, and pendant charm.

2. Unroll a length of flexible wire from the spool. Remember, don't cut the wire—use the spool itself as a "stop." If you have a piece of

precut wire, tie one end in a loose knot and wrap a bit of masking tape over it to form a "stop."

3. Lay out the beads and charms of the main circlet in order, keeping in mind that you will be starting and ending at the top of the pendant.

4. Choose which side to start on. (It doesn't matter in terms of technical reasons, but you may have symbolic reasons for preferring to begin with one side or the other of your design.)

5. String the beads and charms of the main circlet.

6. Check every so often to make sure that all of the beads are in the correct order, and everything is working out properly.

7. When you've strung the entire main circlet, measure the length of the pendant from the place where it joins the main circlet of the rosary to the top of the pendant charm. Add four inches to that figure.

8. The resulting number is the length of flexible wire you need to have on each end of the beads of the main circlet, in order to finish the piece. Measure that amount of flexible wire on both ends of the main circlet. Now cut the wire free from the spool, making sure to leave the full finishing allowance on both ends. Also make sure none of your beads fall off of the wire! If you started with a precut piece of wire, snip off the tape-and-knot "stop."

9. Lay the two lose ends of the flexible wire side by side. Thread the beads of the pendant onto both wires at once, sliding them carefully along the double wire until they rest snugly against the beads of the main circlet. Tug gently and evenly at both ends of the wire, to take up any slack in the main circlet.

10. Now thread your crimp beads onto both wires at once.

11. Thread both wires through the shank (loop) of the pendant charm. Turn them back to form a loop, from which the pendant charm will hang.

Pagan Prayer Beads

12. Slip both wires back through the crimp beads, and if possible though at least one bead above the crimps. Pull the ends gently until the loop of wire around the shank of the pendant charm is just big enough for the charm to move around freely within it.

13. Check the rosary quickly to make sure there's no exposed wire anywhere along its length. If there is any, push the pendant beads more

Hiding the Knot

Having cleverly placed your knot next to a charm or a bead with a large stringing hole, you're in a perfect position to hide the knot inside that bead or charm. How do you do this? Easy. Begin by making sure you leave long loose ends of stringing material on the knot when you tie it. After you've put a drop of glue on the knot and the glue has dried for at least an hour or until no longer tacky to the touch, get out your spare wire needle. (This is one of the many reasons why a spare wire needle is a very useful thing to have.) Take the long loose end of stringing material which is farthest away from the bead or charm you've chosen to use to hide the knot, and thread your wire needle with it. Run the stringing material back through several beads on the side of the circlet away from the chosen bead, pushing the needle out between two beads while you still have some of the loose end left. Free the needle from the end of your stringing material, and snip off the loose end. Now go back to the knot and thread the second loose end through your needle. Run the stringing material back through the chosen bead and several more beads beyond it, and again free your needle, leaving a loose end of the stringing material at least $1/2$ long. *Do not* snip off this loose end. Instead, grab it and tug gently away from your chosen bead. The knot should slip neatly inside the bead, leaving no visible trace. Once the knot is securely inside the bead and you are satisfied that it's properly hidden, *then* snip off the remaining loose end of stringing material. Voilà—one hidden knot.

snugly against the main circlet and pull the wire ends to bring the slack through the pendant. Also check one last time to make sure everything is the way you want it to be—this is the last chance to change anything without starting over with new wire.

14. Once you're sure the rosary is ready to finish, crush the crimps and trim the loose ends of the wire.

For pendant rosaries strung on silk cord or waxed linen thread:

These are the most complicated form of rosary to string, but once you finish one you'll agree it's worth the effort. Although the sequence of steps below may look daunting, it's not actually that complex. We broke it down into short, simple segments to make it easier to follow.

1. Assemble your beads, charms, and pendant charm.

2. Lay out the beads for the main circlet. Put them in the order specified in the design, or in the order of your choice if you are creating your own design.

3. Choose a starting and ending point for the stringing process, keeping in mind where you want to hide the knot. It's best to have the knot somewhere in the section of the circlet which is opposite to the pendant, since this minimizes stress on the knot.

4. Lay out the pendant separately, in one of the bead board's compartments, with the beads in the required order.

5. Prepare your stringing material. If you are using cord that comes on a card with a woven-in needle, unwrap all but the last loop of it from the card. Leave the last loop anchored to the card to give you a knotting allowance. If you are using another thread, unroll a length of thread from the spool, but do not cut it. You want to have plenty of margin for error. If you are using a length of thread or cord that is already cut, tie a "stop" to the loose end of the thread, leaving

Want to use a donut bead for the lowest item in a pendant? Create a seed bead loop on which to hang it. String enough seed beads to go through the donut and loop closed around it, plus one. Pass the strung seed beads through the center of the donut, then pass the stringing material back through the top-most seed bead of the sequence to neatly close the loop. Run the stringing material back up through the beads of the pendant and continue stringing the rest of the rosary. Figure 4-5 shows a close-up of a donut bead strung this way.

Figure 4-5.
An elegant and practical way to string a donut-bead pendant, using seed beads.

yourself two to three inches of thread beyond the "stop" for a knotting allowance.

6. If you are using thread with a woven-on needle, you're ready to go now. Otherwise, thread your needle, leaving about three inches of thread doubled back on itself. Do not double the thread along its entire length as is often done in sewing, because this may make your thread too thick to string the rosary correctly.

7. Run your needle through the first several beads. Let them slide down to the far end of the thread. String a few more beads, allowing them to join the others.

Crimp Beads

Some first-time beaders are scared by crimp beads, but really they're quite easy to use. Follow these five tips and you'll find that using crimp beads is simple and straightforward!

- Use the appropriate number of crimp beads for your project, based on the weight of the item. For a light small rosary such as a hair-dangle, one per closure is usually enough. For a medium-sized, medium-weight piece, two are fine. For a large or heavy piece, three is a good choice. When in doubt, use one more than you think you need and you'll be fine.

- Use the correct size of crimp beads for your stringing material. If you use one of the two finest grades of beading wire, use tiny crimp beads; if you use the heavier grades of beading wire, use the larger crimp beads. Tiny crimps will damage thicker beading wire, if they go on at all; big crimps won't hold fine beading wire.

- Once you've crimped (crushed) the crimps, there's no going back; all you can do is cut the beading wire and start again with a fresh piece and more crimp beads. Therefore, be sure before you crimp that you've got everything right.

- Be sure to scoot your crimp beads up against one another before crimping, instead of letting them spread out along the beading wire as they're prone to do; this gives maximum strength to the resulting closure.

- Make sure you don't catch one of your rosary beads, or the shank of your charm or clasp, in the jaws of the pliers when you crush the crimp beads. If you do, you'll have a broken bead, clasp, or charm on your hands. Even apparently solid metal shanks can smash or twist like warm butter under the pressure exerted by pliers in action.

8. Hold up the rosary to check your progress. Make sure everything is working the way you want it to work.

9. Repeat steps 7 and 8 until you have threaded all of the beads to one side of the pendant. Check the beads carefully; is everything where it should be, and nothing missing? Do you see any places that don't look right? Now, before you string the pendant, is the best time to correct those.

10. If you need to fix or change something, lay the rosary down in the groove of the bead board and slide the thread out of the portion you need to unstring to get to the error. Correct the error and restring the beads until you get back to where you were, and then continue on. Once you are satisfied with everything on the first side of the rosary, proceed to the pendant.

11. Thread the beads of the pendant in the order given for the design, or in the order you have worked out for your own design. (If you have pre-threaded the pendant as discussed earlier in this chapter, you will of course need to remove the beads from that thread, a few at a time.)

12. Run the needle through the shank (loop) of the pendant charm. Then take the needle *back through* the bead above the pendant charm, forming a loop of thread that the pendant charm will hang from.

13. Pull any loose thread through the adjoining bead so your pendant charm is snug up against this bead. Don't string the pendant charm so tightly that the pendant is rigid, but don't let more than $1/16$ inch of thread be visible here. Remember that exposed thread is weakened thread, and may wear enough with handling to break.

14. With your pendant charm secured, run the needle back though the other pendant beads until you have gone back through the bead that started the pendant. Properly done, this means that all of the beads of the pendant are strung on a doubled thread, ending in a loop which holds the pendant charm.

15. Before going on, check to make sure the pendant charm is still strung properly up against the beads, with no areas of thread gapping. Also check to make sure the needle went through all of the spacer beads, instead of around them as can sometimes happen.

16. Hold up your rosary to see how it looks. It's pretty exciting to see it taking shape, isn't it? Examine the pendant to be sure it's working properly and you're satisfied with it. If you want to correct anything in it, now's the time; once you start back up the second side of the circlet, corrections will be much harder to make.

17. If everything is properly strung up to this point, then you want to continue up the other side of the rosary. Repeat steps 7 and 8 until all beads and charms are strung.

18. Now is the time for the final check before finishing. Look carefully, because if you have to correct an error after the thread has been knotted off, you will need a new length of thread to restring the rosary. If you spot an error, unstring and restring the beads by the same method described above and then give everything one final check before continuing.

19. Once you're sure the rosary is entirely the way it should be, it's time to finish it. Hold the rosary up with the loose ends of thread at the top, allowing all of the beads to fall down the thread until they are touching one another and there is no loose thread visible. Give it a gentle shake and tug lightly on the ends of the thread to make sure all of the beads are properly seated.

20. Now lower the rosary to a level, firm surface, letting it lie flat in a V-shape without any part of it overlapping any other part. Bring the two loose ends of thread together and tie a single knot with them, pulling it carefully and slowly to bring the rosary into a closed loop.

21. When the beads or bead and charm touch one another and no loose thread is visible between them, pull the first knot just a little tighter.

Silk cord will stretch a bit, and this step will stretch the thread far enough to ensure a clean closure but not so far that the thread will be weakened.

22. When you have finished the first knot, make sure the rosary remains flexible, capable of draping across your hand. It should not be rigid. If it is, you have strung it too tightly and you will need to loosen the knot a little so the beads have just enough space to shift slightly on the thread. The basic rule is that there should be no thread visible when the rosary is lying flat. You may see very small areas of exposed thread when you pick the rosary up, but this is not a problem.

23. If you picked up the rosary to check it, then you will need to tighten the first knot again because it will have loosened. Once you are sure the rosary is strung with the proper tightness, tie a second knot over the first. Tug the second knot gently but firmly to make it snug against the first knot. If you are using silk, you may feel a "bite" as the second knot settles. This is a good thing; it means that the two knots have pulled the strands of the silk together, which makes your knot stronger and more secure. If you have used waxed linen thread,

Choosing Your Stringing For More Than Strength

Your stringing material can add to the beauty and symbolism of your finished rosary. If any of your selected beads are clear enough to allow stringing material to show through, if you are knotting the stringing material between beads, or if you will have a place in the pendant where the stringing material will show, co-ordinate the color of stringing material with the color of the beads—or use a symbolically appropriate color of stringing material, such as green for earth or blue for water. Even beading wire comes in an astonishing array of colors these days, giving you lots of options.

or if you feel the beads are heavy enough to require a third knot in the silk, tie a third knot.

24. Hold up the rosary and make sure there is no more than ⅛ inch of exposed thread anywhere. If you see too much exposed thread, use a sewing needle to pick the knots apart and retie them more tightly.

25. Now it's glue time. Get your adhesive and a piece of facial tissue. Carefully put a small drop of adhesive onto the knot. Try to cover the knot on all sides with a fine layer of the adhesive. Also try not to get the adhesive on the beads or charms! If it does get on them, or if you end up with too much adhesive on the knot, wipe off any excess with the tissue.

26. Now hold up the rosary by the loose ends of thread, keeping the knot clear of the bead and/or charm to either side of it. Blow gently on the adhesive to speed its drying. This will keep the knot from becoming glued to the bead or the charm, which is preferable because the rosary will last longer if the adjoining beads can move freely and not tug at the knot every time you handle them. If the knot insists on ending up glued to something, though, which does happen sometimes, it's not the end of the world.

27. Once your adhesive is dry on the surface of the knot, which takes usually about five to seven minutes, lay your rosary down and let the adhesive dry for at least another hour.

28. Then you're ready for the final finish: the ends of the thread. You can cut them once the knot is securely glued, or you can thread them back through the beads to either side. Clare prefers to thread them back through, which keeps the knot stronger. If the rosary is strung snugly, the threaded-back ends seldom work free.

29. To run them back through, take a loose wire needle and thread it with one of the ends. Make the doubled-back portion of thread as

Want to use a big bead for the final item in a pendant? Find a smaller bead that works with it and put it below the big bead, using a seed bead if needed to close the bottom. Or just use a seed bead, if the stringing hole in the big bead is small enough. Run your stringing material down through the pendant, ending with the seed bead. Now treat the seed bead as though it were the shank of a pendant charm. Instead of taking the stringing material back through the seed bead, thread it through the bead above the seed bead and back up through the pendant. Continue stringing the rosary.

short as possible. Run the needle back through the beads on that side of the knot until the thread runs out and the needle pulls free. If a short end of thread is left, snip it away. Now repeat on the other side. Your rosary is done!

Troubleshooting While Stringing

A few problems may arise during the stringing process. The most common is to find out the hard way that one of your beads has a blocked stringing hole. With glass, metal, or stone beads, you simply have to throw the bead out and take another. (This is one of the many reasons to buy one or two extra when you shop.) With wood, horn, or bone beads, the hole may be blocked with loose debris that can be blown out, pushed through with a sewing needle, or cleared away by the narrow end of a bead reamer or needle-nosed file.

Another problem is common to poorly drilled stone beads: a stringing hole with a narrow or rough area inside it. Never force stringing material through a bead like this, because the rough area abrades the stringing material and weakens it, resulting in breakage later. Even the heaviest grade of beading wire can be badly damaged if forced through a roughly drilled stone bead. Clare has had rosaries break from their own weight during the final part of the stringing process because of such damage.

You may also find out the hard way that your stringing material is a bit too thick to pass twice through one of the beads on your pendant. If the bead is made of glass, wood, or bone, you can try to finesse the material through a second time; it's not too likely to be damaged or break as a result. However, if you have to pull hard, then your best bet is to replace the bead in question with one that has a larger stringing hole. If you don't have a replacement, try restringing the rosary on the next-thinner grade of stringing material.

Finally, you may sometimes have a glass bead crack during the stringing process, even though no apparent stress was placed on it. Normally, this occurs when the bead has stressed areas, and it would have broken soon in any case. Replace the bead and continue stringing.

Restringing a Rosary

Now comes the time to face an unpalatable fact of life: rosaries break. No matter how carefully you string them, how gently you handle them, how neatly you store them, a rosary that is used and not simply left lying on your altar is going to break sooner or later. You can do a lot to make this happen *later* rather than *sooner*. Choosing a strong, durable stringing material, checking your beads for sharp edges and rough stringing holes, handling the rosary gently and not tugging on it or pulling it taut, and keeping your rosary dry will all lengthen its lifespan. But no matter how careful you are, some day you will have to restring your rosary—either before it breaks, or after.

Before it breaks? Yes. Check your rosary regularly for signs of wear to the stringing material. Often, you'll find that you can see areas of stretched, roughened, or discolored stringing material between beads. Some degree of discoloration is normal around metal beads and the shanks of charms, and some stretching is normal for silk and other natural stringing materials. But any area of stringing material that looks damaged probably is damaged.

Likewise, if you feel an unusual degree of shift in the beads when you pick up the rosary, and it isn't newly strung enough for the thread to still be stretching a little, that probably indicates damage. The challenge, of course, is figuring out how much damage is enough to warrant restringing. That depends on details such as how often you handle your rosary and under what circumstances. If you keep it on your altar and pick it up only to pray with it,

Wire-needle Woes

Wire needles bend easily, and woven-in wire needles usually have kinks in them on purchase due to having been wrapped around a card. Is your needle bent and kinked to the point you're afraid it won't go through your beads? Don't worry. Use your fingertips or the needle-nosed points of your jeweler's pliers to gently straighten the kinked areas of wire. You won't be able to get the angles completely straight, but you should be able to straighten them enough for the needle to work properly.

Always be gentle when straightening curves or kinks in the wire, however. If you pull hard, your needle will end up with a severe curve that will be fairly difficult to straighten out again. This doesn't matter much with small beads, but if you're using larger beads, you can be stuck having to set a badly curved needle aside for a new one.

What if your wire needle won't go through the bead, and isn't bent? Turn the bead around and try putting the needle through the other end first. In Clare's experience, nine times out of ten this solves the problem. Some beads, especially those made of natural materials, have slightly uneven stringing holes, and the needle may hit an invisible lip of bead material when going through in one direction that it can readily pass by when going through in the other direction.

you could let a mild amount of wear and tear go for some time before you need to deal with it to prevent breakage. On the other hand, if your rosary lives in your pocket and you handle it while sitting at the bus stop or hiking in the woods, any visible damage is enough to warrant repair. An unexpected break that sends beads flying into the street or down a trail is a situation you want to avoid.

When you notice a degree of damage that you think requires attention, get out your bead board and all the items you need to restring—wire needles, glue, scissors, stringing material, crimps, pliers, etc. If the stringing material you originally used wore out too quickly, now is a good time to replace it with something stronger—either a heavier grade of the same type of material or a different material that has more tensile strength. You might also want to check and see if the stringing material frayed more severely near a specific bead, then check that bead for rough edges, a cracked lip, or other damage that may have contributed to the break. The bead may need to be repaired or replaced.

When you are ready to begin, lay the rosary in the groove of the bead board and carefully snip the stringing material near the original closure. Take one side of the rosary and move it around the curve of the board so it lies in the groove on the other side, preserving the structure of the rosary intact. Slowly and gently pull the stringing material out of the beads, letting them slide off into the groove of the bead board. Be particularly careful with the pendant, as it can have a life of its own and move in unexpected directions, suddenly sending beads flying. As the pendant comes unstrung, try to catch its beads in the palm of your hand and set them into one of the compartments of your bead board.

The unstringing finished, your next step is to check and make sure the beads and charms are all in the proper order, as they were when you originally strung the piece. Then restring the rosary as you originally strung it.

Repair after breakage, of course, is more challenging than repair before breakage. Usually, you have loose beads to cope with and, in most cases, you also need to reconstruct parts of the design. However frustrated and upset you may be about the breakage, try to stay calm. Collect as many of the original beads and charms as you can find, and lay them out on your bead board in as close to the original order as you can.

Check for missing beads and charms. If you have replacements on hand, insert them into the sequence of beads as needed. If you don't have replacements on hand, take a few minutes to think about other beads you could use instead. Then go shopping to see if you can replace the missing beads with duplicates. If you can't find exactly the same beads, you may already have some ideas in mind about other beads that may fit your needs. Look for these instead. Back home, fill in the gaps with the beads you've bought and look to see if you want to do any redesigning before you go on. Once you're satisfied with what you have, restring the rosary.

Another possibility exists for restringing, of course: choosing to deliberately restring the rosary for some purpose other than repair. Maybe you've found that your rosary is the wrong size to fit comfortably in your pocket, or you realize in retrospect that you want to change the design slightly, or yesterday you found a bead you really wish you'd had sooner so you could have included it. Or maybe the rosary was made for a specific reason, has fulfilled its purpose, and now you want to use some of the beads for something else. All of these are perfectly good reasons to take a rosary apart and restring it. They all involve designing or redesigning the piece, however, so your best bet is to start by brainstorming, as described in chapter 2, to get some ideas for where you want to go with the rosary or with the beads you'll be taking out of it. Once you've worked out the design changes or new design, then you can go forward from there. Redesigning a rosary can be as exciting as designing it the first time!

5

Druid Rosaries

D RUIDRY IS ONE of the fastest-growing branches of the modern pagan movement. Inspired by the ancient Druids, the priests and wizards of the ancient Celts, its roots as a living tradition lie in two places—the Druid Revival of the 18th and 19th centuries and the Celtic Reconstructionist movement of the late 20th century. Like other pagan religious movements, both branches of the Druid movement offer diverse traditions, teachings, and practices. The following rosaries are just two of the countless possibilities for modern Druids.

The Four Elements Rosary

The Druid rosary of the Four Elements was originally designed by John Michael. Clare later revised and expanded the design when she created the first example. This rosary gives practitioners in the Druid Revival tradition a

versatile tool for working with the dance of meanings that surround the four elements, the four seasons, and the eight great festivals of the Druid year. The design includes beads that represent the four elements of the neo-pagan and Druid Revival traditions—air, fire, water, and earth. Echoing the elements themselves, these sequences of beads come together at a bead of spirit that leads down into the pendant.

The pendant consists of a second, larger spirit bead, one bead for each of the four elements, a final spirit bead, and a tree charm representing the multicultural concept of the Tree of Life. The beads are spaced for easy handling by stringing small beads between the primary beads. Five metal charms, representing the four seasons and the undying presence of spirit, are inserted into the design: a feather for spring, a flower for summer, a leaf for autumn, an acorn for winter, and an ivy leaf for that which endures through all seasons.

The beads are grouped in four octads (series of eight) to represent the eightfold Wheel of the Year in each of the four elements. They combine to make a circle of thirty-three beads that represents the thirty-three chief gods of the ancient Celts. Counting the pendant, the design includes a total of nine beads for each of the four elements and a total of three beads for spirit, because the numbers three and nine were of great importance to the ancient

Figure 5-1. Two examples of the Four Elements Rosary.

Celts. The number three is also the number of the Druid elements—nwyfre (spirit), gwyar (flow), and calas (solidity)—and the parent number of the numbers nine and thirty-three.

It's easy to use the details of the beads and charms available to you to add your own personal significance to the basic design. For example, Clare wanted to use carnelian for her fire octad because of the significance that stone has to her, but she was unable to find round red carnelian beads. Instead, she decided to use carnelian rondelles that were easy to locate. This resulted in the octad of fire beads in her personal rosary being significantly shorter than the octads of the other three elements. Clare chose to use this difference as a deliberate symbol of the way summer always seems to pass by in the blink of an eye.

You can also choose materials available to you, as well as concepts and images that are important to you. Do you like the mottled greens of leopard-skin jasper for earth, with sandy-brown picture jasper for the spacer beads? Does a set of glass beads marbled pale blue and white seem perfect for air? Would you prefer a gold charm shaped like a spray of pine needles over a bronze leaf? Have you found a pendant charm shaped like an evergreen tree that appeals to you more than the conventional tree charm next to it? Do you want to use the same spacer beads for the entire rosary, or do you want to use different spacers for each octad?

When making these choices, remember one important point: even if you are following the design we have outlined, the end product will be a rosary that is unique to you—and that is exactly as it should be. Enjoy choosing the beads and charms that call to you. Enjoy the pleasure of creating something that is yours alone.

Materials List

To make your own Druid rosary of the Four Elements, you will need:

- 9 "air" beads, approx 10–12mm

- 9 "fire" beads, approx 10–12mm

- 9 "water" beads, approx 10–12mm

- 9 "earth" beads, approx 10–12mm

- 2 medium-sized "spirit" beads, approx 14mm

- 1 large "spirit" bead, approx 16–24mm

- at least 55 spacer beads, approx 4mm, or size-6/0 seed beads (seed beads are usually sold by the hank or by the bottle, which gives you lots of extras to play with)

- 5 charms (feather, flower, leaf, acorn, ivy leaf)

- 1 tree pendant

- flexible wire

- crimp beads

- scissors

- pliers

- a bead board or mat

Making the Rosary

These instructions are based on the use of flexible wire to string the rosary. Assemble all of your beads. Lay them out in the groove of the bead board, in the following order:

- 2 spacer beads

- the feather charm

- 2 spacer beads

- 8 "air" beads, with a single spacer bead between each (7 spacer beads in all)

- 2 spacer beads

- the flower charm

- 2 spacer beads

- 8 "fire" beads, with a single spacer bead between each (7 spacer beads in all)

- 2 spacer beads

- the autumn-leaf charm

- 2 spacer beads

- 8 "water" beads, with a single spacer bead between each (7 spacer beads in all)

- 2 spacer beads

- the acorn charm

- 2 spacer beads

- 8 "earth" beads, with a single spacer bead between each (7 spacer beads in all)

- 2 spacer beads

- the ivy-leaf charm

- 2 spacer beads

- 1 of the medium-sized spirit beads, turned sideways (to indicate the beginning of the pendant)

Now lay out the pendant separately, in one of the bead board's compartments, with the beads in the following order:

- 1 spacer bead

- the large spirit bead

- 1 spacer bead

- 1 "air" bead

- 1 spacer bead

- 1 "fire" bead

- 1 spacer bead

- 1 "water" bead

- 1 spacer bead

- 1 "earth" bead

- 1 spacer bead

- the other medium-sized spirit bead

- 1 spacer bead

- the tree pendant charm

Assemble your tools: flexible wire, pliers, scissors, etc. Take a couple of minutes to review the material in chapter 4 on how to string rosaries with pendants (see page 89). Prepare your stringing material as described in chapter 4, then double-check your beads and charms to make sure they are laid out properly. If you find any errors, correct them. (Remember, this is the easiest time to fix a mistake!) Now you're ready to start stringing.

1. Run your wire through the beads and charms of the main circlet, in the order given above. Proceed with your stringing until you have threaded the ivy leaf and the two spacers that follow.

2. String the pendant, following the general rules given in chapter 4. Thread the medium-sized spirit bead onto your paired wires, followed by the beads of the pendant in the order listed above. End with two crimp beads.

3. Pass both wires through the shank (loop) of the tree charm. Then take the wires *back through* the crimp bead above the tree, and if possible back through at least one or two other beads as well. Pull any loose wire through the spacer bead so your tree pendant is close to the crimps. Don't string it so tightly that the pendant is rigid, but don't let more than ⅛ inch of wire remain visible here.

4. Check the rosary to make sure everything is right. Once you're sure it's ready for the final step, crush the crimp beads and trim the loose ends of the wire.

The Three Realms Rosary

Just as the rosary of the Four Elements was created for the use of Revival Druids, so the Three Realms rosary was created for followers of Celtic Reconstructionism and other non-revival Druidic traditions. Clare began to develop the design shortly after the Four Elements rosary was completed, and finalized the details after many philosophical debates with her friend Peter McDowell, whose practice looks back to the ancient Celtic cultures by invoking the three realms of land, sea, and sky instead of the four elements. The Three Realms rosary is a tool to work with the energies and imagery of this traditional cosmology.

The design includes beads to represent each of the realms, with spacers chosen to echo the unique characteristics of each realm. Three metal charms complete the symbolism: an acorn for land, a shell for sea, and a feather for sky. Unlike the rosary of the Four Elements, however, the Three Realms rosary has no spirit beads and no pendant. Its design is a simple circlet.

The rosary's beads are grouped in three *enneads* (series of nine), reflecting the importance of these two numbers in traditional Celtic cultures. This is echoed by the three charms and thirty-six spacer beads. The total number of beads and charms in the rosary add up to sixty-six, a multiple of the great parent number three. The variant form of the design, with thirty spacer beads, adds up to sixty beads total, another multiple of three.

Figure 5-2. Two examples of the Three Realms Rosary.

Other details of the design are also symbolic of ancient beliefs. To the Celtic people, the boundary between one realm and another was an intensely magical place, a *liminal* space or threshold where the normal rules are suspended and the Other World holds sway. One Irish hero who was trying to elude his enemies was advised to carry with him always a sack of sand and another sack of heather. This was so he might confuse people inland by saying he had slept with his head on the sea's sands the previous night, and while near the seashore he might create a similar confusion by saying he had slept with his head pillowed on heather. This gave him the appearance of being able to travel impossible distances, but actually he was engaging in an act of threshold magic. To emphasize this liminal quality in the places where two of the three realms join, the charms in the Three Realms rosary are placed between spacer beads from their own realm and spacer beads from the adjacent realm. Thus each realm stands in connection with the next, and each charm resides on the threshold, in liminal space. This will be reflected in some of the sample workings given for this rosary later in this book.

With the Three Realms rosary, as with any design found in this book, you can gain a great deal from adding your own personal significance to the finished piece through your choice of beads and charms. In the first Three Realms rosary Clare made, which was a gift for her friend Peter, she chose stones and spacer beads that were of special importance to him. You can readily do the same for your own piece. What represents water most clearly to you? Blue sodalite, with its white streaks, like foam on the ocean? Cobalt-blue glass beads molded in the shape of raindrops? Shells from a Hawaiian necklace? Once you have chosen your water beads, what spacers look and feel right to go with them? Natural seed pearls? Silver-lined sea-green seed beads? "Liquid silver" beads, which are faceted and twisted to make light run along them in a way that looks like water flowing? Have fun making your choices—and don't forget to handle your preferred beads to see how they feel between your fingers.

Materials List

To make your own Druid rosary of the Three Realms, you will need:

- 9 "land" beads, approx 10–12mm

- 9 "sea" beads, approx 10–12mm

- 9 "sky" beads, approx 10–12mm

- 10 to 12 spacer beads for "land", approx 4mm or size 6/0

- 10 to 12 spacer beads for "sea", approx 4mm or size 6/0

- 10 to 12 spacer beads for "sky", approx 4mm or size 6/0

- 3 charms (feather, shell, acorn)

- stringing material

- wire needles

- a bead board or mat

- a neutral-PH PVA craft adhesive

Making the Rosary

Assemble all of your beads. Lay them out in the groove of the bead board, in the following order:

- the shell charm

- 2 "land" spacer beads

- 9 "land" beads, with a single "land" spacer bead between each (8 spacer beads in all)

- 2 "land" spacer beads

- the acorn charm

- 2 "sky" spacer beads

- 9 "sky" beads, with a single "sky" spacer bead between each (8 spacer beads in all)

- 2 "sky" spacer beads

- the feather charm

- 2 "sea" spacer beads

- 9 "sea" beads, with a single spacer bead between each (8 spacer beads in all)

- 2 "sea" spacer beads

These instructions assume a rosary strung on silk cord or linen thread. If you choose to string the rosary on beading wire instead, select one of the charms as the location for your closure. Or if you're feeling unconventional, string each set of nine primary beads on its own short section of beading wire and fasten each section to the shanks of the charms on either side.

Assemble your tools, and take a few minutes to review the general instructions given in chapter 4 for stringing a rosary without a pendant (see page 80). Prepare your stringing material, double-check your beads and charms, and you're ready to start.

1. Run your needle through the shell charm and the first two seed beads. Let them slide down to the far end of the thread.

2. String the land beads and spacers, allowing them to join the others at the far end of the thread.

3. String the next two spacers, the acorn, and the two spacers after that. Proceed with your stringing until you have threaded all of the beads and spacers onto your stringing material.

4. Hold up your rosary to see how it looks. Make sure there are no empty spaces between beads, and that the beads hang and drape smoothly. Check the design to make certain everything is in the right place, no beads or spacers are missing, etc. If everything is properly strung up to this point, you're ready to finish.

5. Follow the general instructions given in chapter 4, hiding your knots inside the shank of the shell charm once the adhesive is dry (see page 91).

Alternatives

Both of these designs call for specific elements that may not be available to you, that may be outside of your budget range, or that may not be what you want to incorporate into your personal Druid rosary. What are some alternatives?

One of the rosaries in Figure 5-1 (see page 105) was made of stone beads, the other of glass. You can use beads of different materials for each octad: wood for air, glass for fire, shell for water, and stone for earth. Instead of using the conventional yellow/air, red/fire, blue/water, green/earth symbolism, you can choose colors that feel right to you: perhaps white for air, orange for fire, green for water, and black for earth. If you don't like or can't get one or more of the charms, either substitute others or use beads in place of the charms. One of the Three Realms rosaries in Figure 5-2 is made entirely of beads (see page 111); Clare substituted a mother-of-pearl bead and two stone beads for the three charms.

Of course, you can make alterations to the designs themselves, not merely to the materials; review the section on design modification in chapter 2 (see page 42), and go from there. It's surprisingly easy to customize a design for your own needs and preferences.

6

Wiccan Rosaries

W HETHER IT DATES from ancient times as some traditional Wiccans claim, or was created by Gerald Gardner in the 1940s as others suggest, Wicca is far and away the most popular modern pagan tradition and has had a central role in making pagan spirituality a living option for people today. The rich and creative diversity of today's Wiccan traditions make generalization risky, but most Wiccans revere two divine powers—the Triple Goddess and the Horned God—and celebrate their dance of relationship around the turning Wheel of the Year.

We have seen a range of designs for Wiccan rosaries over the past two years while researching and writing this book. These include several variations on the themes of the thirteen lunar months of the year, the Triple Goddess, the eight *sabbats*, and the Horned God, as well as beaded versions of the Wiccan Ladder. The creativity that members of the Wiccan community have put into these rosaries is impressive! Rather than copy any of the designs we have seen, we attempted to create variations on three of these

themes. We chose, for the purposes of this book, to develop designs for a Thirteen Moons rosary, a Triple Goddess rosary, and a Horned God rosary.

The Thirteen Moons Rosary

Wicca, like many modern pagan religions, encourages devotees to pay attention to the lunar as well as the solar cycles. The Thirteen Moons rosary consists of thirteen round moonstone or mother-of-pearl beads, separated by thirteen groups of thirteen seed beads, each group a different color. Several other Wiccan rosary designs use the Thirteen Moons with spacer beads, but

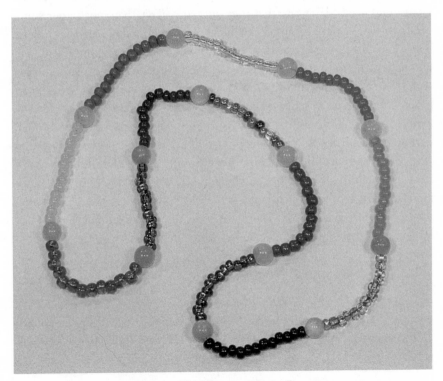

Figure 6-1. The Thirteen Moons Rosary.

each does so in different ways, according to different traditions. The number and color of spacer beads also varies significantly. Some rosaries use the same color beads for each of the thirteen lunar months; others color code the months according to factors such as the "light half" (Belteinne to Samhain) and "dark half" (Samhain to Belteinne) of the year, or the colors of the Triple Goddess. We chose to borrow the color symbolism of Robert Graves' tree calendar, which he in turn borrowed from the color symbolism of the ancient Irish *Ogham* alphabet. Although Graves' calendar is a modern invention, many Wiccans find it useful as a symbolic system. If you prefer to use different colors for your own rosary, see the section on Alternatives at the end of the chapter for suggestions.

One note about shopping for beads for this rosary: If you choose to use moonstone beads, be aware that they are more likely than most other stone beads to have cracks, chips, color flaws, and abnormally narrow stringing holes. You can certainly find thirteen good moonstone beads, but it can be a bit challenging to do so. Be prepared to hunt through the beads on display and, if necessary, buy a strand. With either moonstone or mother-of-pearl beads, Clare suggests you use Superlon thread or the medium grades of flexible wire for stringing. These materials are thin enough to pass readily through narrowly drilled beads. Superlon is a good choice for a votive rosary that won't see much use. If you plan to handle your rosary a lot, flexible wire is strong enough to give it a long working life. If you decide not to use either moonstone or mother-of-pearl, you can easily substitute round, shimmering AB-finish white glass beads. These are lovely and look very moon-like. They also have normal-width stringing holes, which increases the range of possible stringing materials.

Materials List

To make your own Wiccan rosary of the Thirteen Full Moons, you will need:

- 13 white seed beads, size 6/o

- 13 light-grey seed beads, size 6/o

- 13 clear seed beads, size 6/o

- 13 bright-red seed beads, size 6/o

- 13 primrose-yellow seed beads, size 6/o (primrose is a bright, pale yellow)

- 13 purple seed beads, size 6/o

- 13 black seed beads, size 6/o

- 13 dark-grey seed beads, size 6/o

- 13 brown seed beads, size 6/o

- 13 variegated seed beads, size 6/o (use speckled or spotted beads, or use one bead each of thirteen different colors)

- 13 blue seed beads, size 6/o

- 13 green seed beads, size 6/o

- 13 dark-red seed beads, size 6/o

- 13 moonstone or mother-of-pearl beads, size 8–10mm

- charms as desired to incorporate into the design

- stringing material

- wire needles

- a bead board or mat

- a neutral-PH PVA craft adhesive

Making the Rosary

These instructions assume the rosary will be strung on Superlon. If you decide to use flexible wire instead, then you'll need to decide where you're going to put the closure. This would be a rosary where the wire closes on itself, unless you choose to add a charm to the design.

Assemble all of your beads. Lay them out in the groove of the bead board, in the following order:

- moonstone bead

- 13 white beads

- moonstone bead

- 13 light-grey beads

- moonstone bead

- 13 clear beads

- moonstone bead

- 13 bright-red beads

- moonstone bead

- 13 primrose-yellow beads

- moonstone bead

- 13 purple beads

- moonstone bead

- 13 black beads

- moonstone bead

- 13 dark-grey beads

- moonstone bead

- 13 brown beads

- moonstone bead

- 13 variegated beads

- moonstone bead

- 13 blue beads

- moonstone bead

- 13 green beads

- moonstone bead

- 13 dark-red beads

Prepare your materials as described in chapter 4 (see page 80), the section on stringing rosaries without pendants, on thread.

1. String the beads in the order given here.

2. Complete the rosary as described in the general instructions, tying a triple knot to close it.

3. When the glue has dried completely, use the technique given in chapter 4 to hide the knot inside the dark-red seed bead that finishes the thirteenth month (see page 91).

The Triple Goddess Rosary

The Wiccan Goddess may be viewed in many aspects and many moods. Many Wiccans resonate strongly with the Triple Goddess, who resumes in herself the life stages of maiden, mother, and crone. Clare designed a small, simple Triple Goddess rosary that can be used to meditate on these aspects of sacred femininity. Made of moonstone, carnelian, and black onyx beads with glass spacers, it's small enough to tuck into a pocket or purse, yet carries a wealth of meaning.

Figure 6-2. The Triple Goddess Rosary.

Materials List

To make your own Wiccan rosary of the Triple Goddess, you will need:

- 9 moonstone beads, 8mm
- 9 carnelian beads, 8mm
- 9 black onyx beads, 8mm
- 36 clear AB-finish seed beads, approx size 8/0
- 6 silver crimp beads
- beading wire, approx 1 ft, narrow enough to pass through the moonstones

- silver spiral pendant charm

- a bead board or mat

Making the Rosary

Assemble all of your beads. Lay them out in the groove of the bead board, in the following order:

- 3 silver crimp beads

- 3 seed beads

- 9 moonstone beads, with 8 seed beads spaced in between

- 3 seed beads

- 9 carnelian beads, with 8 seed beads spaced in between

- 3 seed beads

- 9 black onyx beads, with 8 seed beads spaced in between

- 3 seed beads

- 3 silver crimp beads

- spiral pendant charm

Prepare your materials and refer to the general instructions in chapter 4 on how to string rosaries on beading wire (see page 85).

1. String the beads in the order given above.

2. Use the closure method that fastens the beading wire to the shank of the pendant charm.

The Horned God Rosary

Many Wiccans find it most appealing to connect to the Wiccan God in his aspect as the Horned God, who is both hunter and hunted, whether they pray to Cernunnos, Pan, or some other aspect of this wild woodland lord. Clare designed a small, simple Horned God rosary to match that of the Triple Goddess. Easily carried in a pocket, it can come with you to any green place for meditation on and communion with the energies of the untamed masculine. It resumes the hunter symbolism in beads of bone, brown wood, and green glass, with a single red bead like a droplet of blood above the stag charm that finishes its short pendant.

Materials List

To make your own Wiccan rosary of the Horned God, you will need:

- 10 flattened round bone beads, approx 10mm
- 6 green glass pony beads, preferably silver-lined (S/L)
- 3 green glass leaf beads, pierced across the top
- 8 dark wood beads, approx 8mm
- 2 dark wood beads, approx 6mm
- 1 dark wood bead, approx 12mm
- 1 red glass teardrop bead
- 6 clear glass seed beads, size 6/0
- 1 stag pendant charm
- stringing material
- wire needles

Figure 6-3.
The Horned
God Rosary.

- a bead board, towel, or plate
- a neutral-PH PVA craft adhesive

Making the Rosary

These instructions assume the rosary will be strung on waxed linen thread. If you decide to use flexible wire instead, follow the instructions for stringing rosaries with pendants and attach the wire to the shank of the stag charm. Use three gold crimp beads to close the wire.

Assemble all of your beads. Lay them out in the groove of the bead board, in the following order:

- 8mm wood bead
- bone bead

- pony bead
- 8mm wood bead
- bone bead
- pony bead
- 8mm wood bead
- bone bead
- seed bead
- leaf bead
- seed bead
- 8mm wood bead
- bone bead
- pony bead
- 6mm wood bead
- 6mm wood bead
- pony bead
- 8mm wood bead
- bone bead
- seed bead
- leaf bead
- seed bead
- 8mm wood bead
- bone bead

- pony bead

- wood bead

- bone bead

- pony bead

- wood bead

- bone bead

- seed bead

- leaf bead

- seed bead

Then lay out the pendant in a separate compartment, in the following order:

- bone bead

- 12mm wood bead

- bone bead

- red glass teardrop bead

- stag pendant charm

Prepare your materials, and use the general instructions for stringing rosaries with a pendant, strung on thread.

1. String in the order given, up to and including the first 6mm wood bead.

2. String the pendant.

3. Resume at the second 6mm wood bead, continuing through the final leaf and seed bead.

4. Finish the rosary as described in chapter 4 (see page 91), using the technique given to hide the knot inside the 8mm wood bead next to the final seed bead.

Alternatives

For the Thirteen Moons rosary, if the Ogham colors for the thirteen months don't appeal to you, consider these options:

- Use white or light-colored seed beads for the "light half" of the year and black or dark-colored seed beads for the "dark half" of the year. Make the switch halfway between moonstone bead #7 and moonstone bead #8.

- Use black seed beads between moonstone beads #1 and #5. Four beads between #5 and #6, switch to white seed beads. Continue with white seed beads through moonstone bead #9. Finally, eight beads between #9 and #10, switch to red seed beads. This resumes the maiden/mother/crone aspects of the yearly cycle.

- Use seed beads of all one color, selecting one that is meaningful to you.

- Use seed beads of whatever colors you wish, depending on your own personal beliefs and preferences.

If you simply find the Thirteen Moons rosary too long, or too complicated, or too expensive to make, there is a simpler form given in chapter 8 (see page 156). This simpler rosary, meant to be worn as a bracelet or hair-dangle, can also be made as a pocket piece by inserting a small charm in place of the bracelet catch and fastening the beading wire to the shank of the charm.

For the Triple Goddess rosary, you could easily select a different pendant charm, or use alternate stones such as mother-of-pearl, red jasper, and amethyst, or just switch to glass beads. Using green seed beads instead of clear ones hints at the Goddess' role in Wiccan lore as the source of all life.

For the Horned God rosary, you could again select a different pendant charm, substitute red-glass beads for the wood beads to represent the Hunter's sacrifice of his own blood, use another shape of green bead in place of the pony beads, replace the leaf beads with more pony beads, or add spacer beads to the design. You can also omit the pendant and insert the stag charm between the two 6mm wood beads to complete the rosary. Or you can omit the entire pendant, including the stag charm, and insert a bone bead in its place to create a very simple circlet rosary. Many changes can be rung on the basic design to make a rosary that is your own expression of how you honor your God.

Special-purpose Rosaries

YOU MAY HAVE MANY REASONS for wanting to make a rosary different from the ones discussed in previous chapters. You may want to honor a specific god or goddess, or memorialize someone who has passed away, or connect with your ancestors. Many occasions in your life or the lives of your friends and loved ones can be commemorated or helped along with a rosary: surgery, a job hunt, marriage, a cross-country move, menarche, retirement, a new baby. As you'll see in chapter 9, rosaries can be more than a medium for prayer or meditation. They can be used as magical tools to focus on an intended goal, to work healing and blessing spells, to protect from harm, to help banish fear and invoke hope, and to fire the heart and memory with love when far from home and family. This chapter explores some of the many possibilities for making rosaries to fulfill these special purposes.

Rosaries for Special Deities

One of the hallmarks of the pagan revival is its multiplicity of gods and goddesses, drawn from a range of traditional pagan pantheons. Most modern pagans work primarily with only a few deities, generally ones to whom they feel a particular connection or by whom they have been called. In some cases, the person has initiated the relationship; in other cases, the deity has done so. But in all cases, the relationship has a special value that sets this deity apart from others.

One of the ways a pagan can honor a personal deity is by making a votive rosary as an offering to that deity. Whether such a rosary lives on your altar or in your pocket, each time you handle it and use it for prayer, meditation, or communion with the deity, you remind both yourself and your special goddess or god how much the relationship means to you, and you make anew

Figure 7-1. Three rosaries for individual deities.
From top to bottom: Pan, Aphrodite, Lugh.

your gift of dedication. If you have more than one personal deity, you can design and make individualized rosaries for all of them, reflecting the unique nature of your connection to each.

How do you make a rosary for a deity? You might wish to begin by reviewing all you know about your goddess' or god's traditional iconography and symbolism. If you feel you don't know enough, do some research in a reputable source. Watch out for material posted on the Internet or included in popular dictionaries of deities; this is often severely flawed and inaccurate. Your best bet is to look up your deity in scholarly books about his or her religion of origin; this material is more likely to be documented and verifiable. When in doubt, try to cross-reference several sources to make sure you have the clearest information you can get. If you can't find anything, or if what you find is contradictory, try the method given in the next paragraph. In any case, take copious notes of what you remember and whatever you can find. Writing it down helps you to clarify the information and organize it mentally, which is an important step in the process.

Next, pray to your goddess or god—light a candle, burn some incense, make an offering, whatever feels right to you or is part of your normal practice with that deity. Ask what he or she wants. Seek guidance. If you were making a gift for a friend or relative you would want to have some idea of what the recipient would like; do the same with your deity. After making your request, sit down and write, or do a divination, or close your eyes and daydream; open the gates to let an answer come through. Listen carefully. It may come to you in the form of words, images, sounds, colors, or scents—a bird flying past you when next you go outside, a tree catching your eye as you look out the window, a sudden call from a friend who wants to talk about something that just happened, a card you turn up. It may come in the form of an impulse to go to the bead store, where you find six beads of this color, five of that shape, twelve of a certain material or design.

Whatever answer you receive, even if it is none at all that you can tell, sit down and make notes on the possibilities. What colors are appropriate to this deity? What materials? What numbers? What symbols? For example, if you are planning a rosary for Brigid, you might choose the numbers three and nine, since these were important to the ancient Irish; consider the colors red, yellow, and orange to represent the flames of her forge, since she was a goddess of smith-craft; perhaps a charm in the shape of a well, since she is associated with a healing well. You may choose to add the color green to represent her general association with healing. Since you have a limited budget right now and don't think you can afford to spend much more than $10, use glass beads. These, then, are the parameters you have chosen to work within: threes and nines; red, yellow, orange, and green; the well. From there, you can work out a design and proceed through the making process.

Rosaries for Ancestors

Many pagan traditions, new and old, place great importance on ancestors, whether by deifying them, revering them, or simply looking to them for protection and aid. Shamanic traditions and traditional faery lore also tend to give ancestral spirits an important place. For all of these reasons and more, many neo-pagans are beginning to look toward working with their ancestors as a desirable practice, and many others already include some form of ancestor work in their normal practice. One of the ways you can work with your ancestors in a positive, reverent manner is by making and using one or more ancestor rosaries.

You can approach the idea of an ancestor rosary from several different angles, depending on your needs and on your family of origin issues. For some people, working with their immediate ancestors is best; they feel warmly supported by their late parents, grandparents, aunts, uncles, and cousins. Other people prefer not to be connected to their immediate family members, and would much rather work with distant ancestors, those whom they never knew in life and of whom they have never heard even vague stories. Still others prefer to work with a mixture of distant and more recent ancestors, or feel a need to connect to ancestors whom they never knew, but who are well represented in the body of family legends. If you come from an abusive family, you may prefer to contact the ancestors of your clan or the collective ancestors of your ethnic background rather than any members of your own blood lineage. All of these combinations, and many more, are possible, and you can readily design ancestor rosaries to represent your own needs and preferences in this matter.

At this point it is perhaps best to deal with the sometimes vexed question of adoption. If you are adopted, you may have little or no information about your birth parents and family, and perhaps no possibility of contact. If you do have contact with members of your birth family, you may feel that you have two families of origin, and wish to work with ancestors from both; or you may feel that your adoptive parents are your "real" family, and it is their ancestors you wish to contact; or you may have had an unpleasant experience with your adoptive family and may wish to work only with ancestors in your birth family, known or unknown. The simple fact is that you may choose whichever of these options works best for you.

In many traditional societies, adoption is considered to make the adoptee a full member of the adoptive family, with all the proper connections to ancestors conferred upon the finalization of the adoption. If you wish to work with the ancestors of your adoptive family, you have this link to draw upon. On the other hand, if you wish to work exclusively with your birth family, you can always ask your deities and/or allies to help you connect with these blood ancestors. If you choose to work with both birth and adoptive families, call upon both blood and ritual ties to aid you in your efforts. Clare has known pagan adoptees who have used each of these three choices, and done well. Or you may choose, as many pagans do, not to take the path of ancestor work; that, too, is a valid option.

Once you have decided to make an ancestor rosary, it's wise to try to establish some form of contact with the ancestors you are honoring and ask for their guidance. If you have an ancestor altar, pray and make offerings at it. If you do not have such an altar, then simply pray to your gods and, through them, to your ancestors. If you do faery work, enlist the aid of your allies in this matter; they are likely to be most eager to assist you. Whatever path of contact you choose, listen for answers and be aware that these may not take the form of words. Having asked your ancestors for guidance, sit down and work through a process similar to the one described for personal deities.

The main difference is that, instead of exploring the known symbolism, legends, and imagery of a deity, you need to decide which level(s) of ancestors you want to work with—distant, recent, all, specific individuals, etc.—and how you want to represent them. If you have ancestors you explicitly wish to avoid working with, such as perhaps an abusive parent or grandparent, make it clear to the ancestors whom you contact that this is the case and ask them to honor that request. Normally, they are more than happy to do so, and they may even provide you with protection against those you wish to avoid.

Let's begin with the idea of distant ancestors, those predating written history in the countries of your family's origin. For example, Clare chose to make a strand representing ancestors from the Neolithic and Bronze Age, periods for which she had ancestor contacts in place. For such a rosary, your best choices for materials are beads made from things readily available in pre-modern times: wood, seeds, nuts, berries, bone, horn, metal, glass, stone, shell, clay. Always look for beads that appear as if they could have been made a long time ago; modern, glossy, plastic, and/or high-tech are the exact opposite of what you want.

If you consider metal beads, for instance, select ethnic-looking beads that could have been made with pre-industrial methods; for instance, simple Thai

Figure 7-2. An example of an ancestor rosary for distant ancestors.
All of these beads could have been made with pre-industrial technology.

hammered silver beads or African *heishi* are among the choices that would work well. If you consider glass beads, don't choose those made of highly re-fined glass molded or cut into complex shapes, but rather somewhat cruder glass; simple beads, especially those with a fire-polish, from the Czech Republic, India, or Egypt have the right sort of look and feel. If you choose clay beads, they should not be delicate ceramics, but made of plain clays or the older, simpler forms of porcelain such as blue-and-white Asian beads. All of these types of beads have existed in some form for thousands of years; this is the flavor you want for a primal ancestor rosary.

In choosing charms for a primal ancestor rosary, look for those that repre-sent natural things: feathers, leaves, pine cones, acorns. Avoid modern designs or items with a mass-produced feel; look for charms that vary a bit from one to another and even have small flaws or rough spots, as handworked items would. Good pendant choices include large, slightly worked stone beads; carved beads of wood, bone, or horn; figurines made from clay, wood, horn, or shell. If you choose to omit a pendant, a few such larger beads can be worked into the body of a circlet rosary. For either charms or pendants, you could seek out representations of any animals you know to which your ancestors had connections, or that you connect to in your ancestor work: hawk, wolf, bear, etc. Appropriate stringing materials for primal ancestor rosaries include thread, string, or cord made of leather, silk, or braided cotton. Avoid modern materials such as rayon, elastic, or tiger-tail.

How many of what sort of beads and charms should you use? This is en-tirely up to you. We have little surviving material explaining what numbers and symbols were important to our ancestors in the periods before written records, and often what we do have is simply the symbols themselves. If you are making a rosary for, say, ancestors who lived in Bronze Age England, you can guess to some extent, but you are only filling in possibilities; there are no certainties. Let your intuition guide you, as well as any responses you receive from your deities and/or ancestors themselves.

What if your goal is to work with more recent ancestors? Sit down with a family tree if you have one, or with your recollections of family stories. Con-sider the ancestors you knew, those you've heard stories about, those whose names grab your attention or stick in your memory. If you can, have a talk with an older member of the family about those members who are now gone, some of whom perhaps you knew only for a few years of your childhood, or perhaps not at all. Even if you knew your grandparents well, your older relatives may know details about their childhoods, their brothers and sisters, their parents, their jobs or country of origin that you don't have. You can begin with your parents and their siblings, and go back as far as possible. Mine the vein of family lore; collect the tall tales as well as the true tales, for even family legends hold a grain of truth. Once you have a sense of who your recent ancestors were, decide whether you want to work with them as a group, or whether you want to connect to select individuals more deeply.

Another point to consider in making a recent ancestor rosary is whether you already have items you may want to incorporate into it. If you have a few beads from your grandmother's jet necklace or from Aunt Hester's eyeglass keeper, perhaps a seal that hung on your great-grandfather's watch fob or a charm from a bracelet your mother had in the eighth grade, these may merit inclusion in the rosary. If you have a pendant your favorite uncle gave you on some long-ago Christmas, perhaps it could be worked in. This is another time to turn to older members of the family, if you feel it's appropriate; Granddad may just turn out to have, lurking among his tie tacks, a beaded earring you remember seeing Grandma wear.

Now think about what you know of the ancestors you're considering working with. Did one come from Russia, fleeing the Revolution? Perhaps one was a 49er in the Gold Rush days, or the captain of a China clipper. How about a woman who homesteaded on the prairie, an herb doctor, or a midwife? Was Great-grandpa a railroad engineer? Did Grandma win blue ribbons for her quilts, or her cherry pie? Did Aunt Eunice or Uncle Bill secretly write poetry? What about your mother's cousin Mabel, who took over the family grocery store and ran it successfully after her husband was killed in the War?

Any or all of these could be incorporated into a rosary. How? Look for beads or charms that call these things to mind: a bead of Siberian jade, a gold nugget or gold-pan charm, a Chinese porcelain bead, a covered wagon charm, or a set of letter beads spelling out the word "baby." You can also incorporate your memories of a recent ancestor whom you knew. Perhaps Granddad's favorite sweater was a certain shade of green, or Great-aunt Harriet loved to tend her roses in the summertime; try to find a bead that's the right green, or a bead with a rose painted on it. Be creative, and look for beads that fire off associations in your mind. If you see a bead when you are shopping that makes you think "Mom," consider buying it to represent your mother. Likewise, if an apparently perfect bead just doesn't feel right, trust your instinct and let it go.

How many of which type of bead or charm should you use? That's up to your own sense of what fits. Was your dad's lucky number six? Then consider having six beads in the rosary to represent him. If Great-aunt Harriet's favorite rose was the five-petaled wild rose, then maybe you'll want to use five rose-pink beads for her. If nobody in your family cared about numbers or patterns, do what feels right to you.

Suppose you decide you want to work with a mixture of distant and recent ancestors. Go ahead and work out some ideas for whom you want to represent, and how. Think about whether you want one type of ancestor or the other to predominate, or whether you want to balance the two. Consider whether you want to divide the rosary up into sections representing the different ancestors, perhaps one half being distant ancestors and the other half recent ones—or whether you want to mingle the different beads. Make some notes; perhaps draw a sketch or two. Consider making an exploratory trip to the bead store; wander around to see what's there; see what ideas are triggered in your creative mind. Here, as always, the key is to enjoy making something that feels right and works for you. If you get stuck, review the hints in chapter 2 to see if they shake something loose.

Memorial Rosaries

Memorial rosaries can commemorate any death or passing: a family member, a friend, a beloved pet, the demolition of the house you used to live in, the cutting of a familiar tree in your favorite park, the closure of the company

Figure 7-3. A memorial rosary.

where your mom worked during your childhood, the clearing of your grand-parents' farm for a housing development. All of these passages and many more can be marked by making and using a memorial rosary.

The design process for such a rosary is fairly simple. If it's a memorial for a person, begin by thinking about what that person would want to see in the rosary; what might that person want to be remembered for, what did he or she like, what would he or she have thought important about his or her life? Then think about what you want to remember about the person, what is important to you to include in the rosary. Review all of your favorite memories, the stories that circulate in the family or among friends, the little things that stick in your mind when a loved one is gone: he liked cake donuts for break-fast; she was famous for her flower garden; he kept a piece of petrified wood on his desk to fiddle with; she watched birds; he was on the track-and-field team in college and won a trophy; she went to France every two or three years.

Fill your mind with memories; fill your heart with that person's spirit. Consider also having an imaginary conversation with the person, or writing down some of your thoughts and letting your memory of the person respond to these as though he or she were reading and commenting on what you've written. With all of this to draw on, go through your collection of mementoes, sort out the beads in your bead box, or go to the bead store and see what feels right. When you've collected the beads you want, use the process described in chapter 4 to finalize your design (see page 77).

If the memorial is for a pet, a wild animal, a tree, or some other non-human living thing, the process is very similar: review your memories, filling your mind and spirit with an awareness of this creature you loved, of what it felt and looked and smelled like, its personality, everything you can remember. From this, look for beads or charms that remind you of the creature—the color of its fur or eyes, the shape of its leaves, anything that captures its spirit and your feelings for it. Then take what you find and work out a design. Are you memorializing a place or thing—a piece of land or a building, a business now closed, or a pond now silted in and breeding a meadow? Again, the key is to review your memories and find beads and charms that represent this place or thing to you.

Other Special Purposes

Any important life event can be marked by a rosary or prayer-bead strand, from the joyful (the birth of a child) to the fearful (a soldier's period of duty in a foreign country during wartime), from the uncertain (founding a new business) to the definite (celebrating retirement). Rosaries can help a mother-to-be get through her labor and welcome her new baby, remind a soldier of his or her family at home and help the family to focus their thoughts and prayers on their loved one's safety, give a new business owner a way to focus on his or her goals among the welter of tasks involved in a startup, welcome a new retiree to a life filled with the possibilities that the demands of work have kept on hold for years.

Give a pair of rosaries to a bride and groom both to commemorate their wedding and to provide them with something on which to focus when they hit bumps in the road and want to keep their marriage strong. When you send your teenager off to college in a distant town, send along a strand of prayer beads to comfort him or her during bouts of homesickness and to trigger memories of your loving support. If you want to help or bless those going through a difficult period, a strand of prayer beads can symbolize your good wishes and give you something you can lay on your altar to remind you to pray for them, something you can hold in your hand to focus on while you gather loving energy to send to them, something you can give them as a tangible vehicle for your blessings and aid.

Aside from blessing and prayer, many other magical tasks can be aided by a rosary. Anything involving repetition is easier to carry out correctly when you have something on which you can count how many times you have repeated the phrase or charm. A strand of beads is ideal for this purpose, and can readily be carried in a pocket or purse, or worn as a bracelet or necklace to help keep the process going all day long. Likewise, anything requiring focus on a goal benefits from having something concrete to use as a tool to aid that focus. A strand of beads designed to remind you of a goal can help you keep it in mind, give you something to hold onto when you are tired or discouraged and need to regain your drive, and provide a meditative tool to help you think your way through obstacles that may arise.

Here are some examples of special-purpose rosaries.

Body-honoring Rosaries

In the modern world, we are all constantly bombarded by messages telling us that our bodies are not good enough. Women are criticized for their breast size and shape, and for showing signs of age, especially grey hair or dry skin. Men are criticized for their penis size, musculature, and hairlines. Both sexes are criticized for their weight, wrinkles, and body odors. Male or female, we are all held up to youthful and impossible standards of beauty.

Many pagans recognize that this is a form of black magic, designed to make people feel inadequate so they will buy products that claim to help us fix our inadequacy. Perhaps this is in part because pagans see the body, not as a vessel of sin and fall from grace that other religions have represented it to be, but rather as a gift from the gods and a source of joy. All the same, having been raised with such black magic beating on us day after day, we still tend to succumb to traces of it. How often have you worried about your weight, about whether you're looking old, about whether someone of the desired sex will see you as attractive? Even if you're generally pretty comfortable with yourself, odds are that, all too often, these worries creep into your thoughts.

Help yourself counter this by designing and making a rosary to honor your body. Use bone beads for your bones; red beads for your blood; beads of whatever color you deem appropriate for your flesh. If you are female, add beads or charms to represent your breasts and vulva; if male, beads or charms to represent your penis and testicles. Think about parts of your body that you love or especially value—your deft and capable hands, your strong legs, your beautiful eyes. Choose a bead or beads to represent each of these. Now think about parts of your body that you especially dislike or hate—your fat tummy, the mole on the back of your right hand, your big ears, your clumsy feet. Choose beads to help you reconcile to these parts and honor them for the good they have within them.

Next, think about sensory or physical experiences that make your body feel good—sex, food, sports, hot baths—anything that your body enjoys and thrives on. Include beads or charms to represent these as well. Finally, select a pendant charm if you wish. If you choose to put a pendant on your body-honoring rosary, consider using one bead each for flesh and blood and bone, a green bead for your body's life force, and a spirit bead to represent your body as a whole. Create your rosary as an act of recognition that, perfect or not, your body is your home and deserves love and care from the spirit that inhabits it.

Sexuality Rosaries

Another aspect of the negative messages we constantly receive about our bodies is the immense amount of propaganda about sex and human sexuality. Whether you are male or female, white or minority, gay or straight, society is all too ready to tell you what you should—or more often should not—do with your genitals, and how often, and with whom. The reality that gets swept away in this torrent of nanny-state legislation and opinion is that human sexuality is as complex, varied, and beautiful as are the millions of flowers with which our green kindreds express their sexuality. Each of us is unique. We have our own special needs and desires, our own truth about who we are and how we choose to express ourselves sexually.

If you are struggling to find yourself sexually, if you need to work on sexual issues, or if you simply wish to honor your own sexuality—whether masculine, feminine, or both—consider creating a rosary that expresses this side of you. Find beads and charms that speak to you of your own needs, desires, and loves, and string them in a pattern you find pleasing. Whenever you need or want to work on this aspect of yourself, whether to develop a clearer sense of what you want or simply to remind yourself that it's okay to be you, handle the rosary; pray, meditate, and explore within yourself using the beads as a vehicle for the journey.

Spell-casting Rosaries

You can also make a rosary for any magical purpose you choose, and use it as a magical working tool. As with any magical working, start by formulating your intention as clearly and precisely as possible. A good working rule is that you should be able to say it in a single sentence that can't be misunderstood in any way. Take your time with this step; let it unfold at its own pace.

Once you know exactly what your intention for the spell will be, decide what sort of rosary symbolizes it best. What color, shape, and size of beads represent your intention? Are there charms or a pendant that will help you focus your magic on this purpose? As with any other rosary, you can make these choices at home, in advance of a trip to the bead store, or you can go straight to the bead store and let inspiration be your guide.

When you have all the beads and other materials you need, gather them together. Before you begin making the rosary, use whatever method you prefer to establish sacred space—if you're Wiccan, for example, cast a circle and call the quarters. Put the rosary together within the circle, concentrating all the while on your intention. When the rosary is finished, put it in a cloth bag. Later, you can consecrate it with the ritual given in chapter 9 (see page 164) or any other ritual you prefer, and use it to focus your mind and will on the spell.

Four Faery Cities Rosary

You work with the faery folk. After consultation with your faery allies, you decide that the focus of your work for the next several months will be the four fabled cities of Gorias, Finias, Murias, and Falias. You've read all the traditional and modern faery lore you can get your hands on. You've found a few elusive bits of information about them and created a clear image of each city and how to journey safely to it. You decide you want to use a rosary to help you in this work. With the help of your allies, you select four large beads, one to represent each city, and a number of smaller beads to represent the various symbols associated with each city. You decide you want to include a pendant in your design, and choose beads for this that represent for you the route by which you travel to a jumping-off point between the cities. You lay out the beads and create a design in which each of the four beads is in the center of its smaller beads, with a triad of seed beads to separate each group from the next. This comes together at the pendant, which you have strung so that it mimics your own inner journey, beginning from the pendant charm and running up the strand of beads to the main circlet.

Once you have assembled the rosary, you begin using it as an aid to your journey work. Holding it quiets your mind and turns your deep attention to the work at hand. Tracing the pendant helps you journey inward to your jumping-off point, and running your fingers over the beads that represent your city of choice brings that city clearly before you in all its wonder. Finally, when you're finished in the city, returning to the pendant and tracing it from the main circlet down to the charm helps you return completely to the outer world.

Ocean Powers Rosary

A vacation on the coast causes you to realize that, although you live too far from the ocean to visit it more than occasionally, you resonate deeply with its energies and want to keep it more present in your life than it has been until now. In a bead store in the small coastal town where you are staying, you find a strand of beads marked "ocean fossil." Talking to the clerk behind the counter, you find out that these stone beads, with their tiny fossil *radiolaria* and other creatures, are actually found in mountains that were once seabed. You buy the beads, feeling the ocean energy that fills them almost to the bursting point. Back in your hotel room, you handle the beads and decide to make a rosary from them. Later on, at home, you find translucent glass beads in various shades of watery blues and greens that remind you of the ocean. You need spacer beads, so you get some quartz-crystal chips that look like

Figure 7-4.
An Ocean Powers Rosary.
The large beads are
ocean fossil.

water droplets, and finish with a few thin stone chips that are made from river pebbles. You string a strand that is so full of ocean energies you can feel the ocean flowing into you every time you touch it. You use your new treasure to work with ocean energies and find that your own energies, fed by the sea, blossom in new directions.

As you can see, the possibilities for special-purpose rosaries are almost endless. Turn your imagination loose, and you can create exactly what you need for your loved ones, your magical work, or your daily life.

8

Rosaries You Can Wear

I T ISN'T ALWAYS CONVENIENT or possible to carry a rosary with you all day long, or to carry one to some evening event. But you may want to continue a practice you're working on that requires repeating a prayer or chant at regular intervals. Or you may have gotten used to running your rosary through your fingers when you need to relax. Or perhaps you may enjoy an extra feeling of closeness to your deity when you have your rosary at hand, but you need to hide your paganism at work, so you can't really use a rosary while at your desk. The wonderful thing about beaded rosaries is that they can easily be made in the form of jewelry you can wear and fiddle with anywhere—even if you need to stay in the broom closet. This chapter explains some of basic jewelry rosary types and how to make them, including how to alter existing designs to fit the parameters of a jewelry design.

Necklace Rosaries

The easiest kind of wearable rosary to make is a necklace rosary. The circlet of a necklace rosary must be long enough to fit around your neck, or, if you would rather not use a clasp, long enough to fit over your head. In most cases, this means the circlet should to be 18 to 24 inches around. It's not unusual for a rosary to be 12 to 18 inches around in any case, so often, the only modification you need to make to an existing design is to extend it the appropriate number of inches to get something that will fit you properly. The simplest ways to do this are by using larger primary beads, by increasing the total number of beads, or by inserting a clasp into the design.

Inserting a clasp works quite well in many designs. For instance, if you want to insert a clasp into an ancestor rosary, just select the beads around the clasp to produce a harmonious, attractive result. In some designs, however,

Figure 8-1. A necklace rosary.

such as the Thirteen Moons rosary, inserting a clasp can be awkward and would leave the resulting piece unbalanced. If you are considering inserting a clasp into a design, sketch out your idea first and see how it works, or lay the beads out on your bead board and check how they look. If you find a place where you think a clasp will fit, great; find a suitable clasp and go ahead with stringing your rosary. If you don't see a way to add a clasp, then consider using the number and size of the beads to achieve the desired length.

Changing the number of beads is very easy to do in some designs. Basically, if the number of beads in the rosary is not important to its symbolism, you can readily find places to add more beads. If the beads are not arranged in a set pattern, just put more beads into places where they fit well and look pleasing. If the beads are arranged in a set pattern, you can either increase the number of beads or increase the number of sets. For instance, if you want to make a necklace-length version of the Triple Goddess rosary (see page 122), you could do three sets each of the onyx beads, three sets each of the moonstone beads, and three sets each of the carnelian beads, using three seed bead spacers between each set of nine. This results in a total of nine sets of nine beads, which is symbolically very appropriate and increases the total loop length from 9½ inches to approximately 29 inches.

If the beads are in set patterns that are symbolically significant, and you don't want to change the number symbolism, try increasing the size of the primary beads. For example, to preserve the eight-fold symbolism in the Druid Four Elements rosary (see page 106–07), you could select beads for the circlet that are 16mm or 18mm wide instead of 10mm. If this doesn't give you quite enough additional length, you could change the size of the spacer beads from 4mm to 6mm or 8mm. (In calculating extra length, remember there are 25.4mm to the inch.) Surprisingly small changes can add up fast, however, so keep track of the total circlet length or, when you make your necklace rosary, you may find it reaches much farther down your chest than you expected!

Do you want a pendant on your necklace rosary? Any changes you make in the total number or size of beads in the circlet is going to affect the proportion of the pendant to the rest of the rosary. This may make a pendant that was perfectly sized for the original design appear absurdly small, or, if you carry out your chosen design changes in the pendant as well as in the circlet, may result in a pendant that is far too long and looks clunky and awkward. You may also find that, for reasons of comfort or general appearance, you don't want a pendant on a necklace rosary. Or, when you lay out your beads, you may find that the design simply cries out for a small pendant to make it look right as a necklace.

Keep these factors in mind when redesigning a rosary into a necklace. Take your time in evaluating whether or not you want to keep a pendant that was already part of the design. If you decide to keep it, put some thought into whether you want to keep its original design and size, or whether you want to change it. For example, in the Druid Four Elements necklace rosary discussed above, you almost certainly do not want to use 18mm primary beads in the pendant, or larger spacers. Instead, you may want to use 14mm beads and 4mm spacers, or perhaps simply have the main spirit bead lead directly to the tree charm and eliminate the remaining pendant beads altogether. Don't hesitate to do a trial stringing of the rosary on ordinary sewing thread so you can hold it up in front of you and see how it's going to look when finished. This can ease any doubts you may have about how your design is going to work, as well as help you spot problems before the rosary is too far along in the actual stringing process.

On the other hand, if you're not using an existing design, you can work around all of these considerations very easily. Simply decide whether you want to use a clasp and, if so, what kind; then create your design. If you do decide to use a clasp, you may find it useful to get the clasp first and design around it. There are some amazing clasps available in bead stores and catalogs, and you may well find something special that makes a design come alive for you. Finally, decide whether you want to use a pendant, or perhaps a pendant charm. Again, this may be something to shop for beforehand, to use as the focus for your design. Just the right thing can spark your creativity to make a beautiful piece that serves as both a devotional tool and a favorite item of jewelry.

Bracelet Rosaries

These small rosaries are a lot of fun to make and wear. The only real challenge you face in creating a bracelet rosary is that you have no more than six to nine inches of total length to work with, so any existing designs must be miniaturized. Once you get used to the scale of the circlet, however, you can really delight in making these little gems.

The basic principles of reducing a rosary to bracelet length are fairly simple. First and foremost, you need to decide whether or not you're going to include a clasp. The whole process of redesign will be affected by this choice. Unlike a necklace rosary, which can safely be slipped over your head, a bracelet rosary loose enough to slip on over your hand may also be loose enough to slip off again, possibly without your noticing it. This means that a bracelet rosary strung without a clasp will either have to be sized to just barely go over your

Figure 8-2. Bracelet rosaries.

hand, or will need to be strung on elastic. Consider both of these options in the design and bead-selection process. No matter which you choose, you'll need to make sure all of your beads are smooth, with no facets or knots that will be uncomfortable to slide over your hand. You may also find it more comfortable to avoid chunky beads. Likewise, if you choose a clasp, take into account what kind of clasp will work best for you—something that can be worked one-handed, like a bar-and-toggle clasp, or the classic spring ring and jump ring combination. What styles and sizes are available in the type of clasp you want? A trip to your bead store may be in order to evaluate your choices before you settle your final design.

The choice made about whether or not to use a clasp, your next step is to evaluate the rosary design and decide what's most essential to its spirit. For example, in the Thirteen Moons rosary (see page 118–19), the number thirteen is the essential symbol. Therefore, a redesign of it as a bracelet should retain the thirteen primary beads. You can easily retain the symbolism of using moonstone for these. Since thirteen beads, especially 10mm beads, won't be long enough as a bracelet by themselves, you'll still need spacers. You can use 4mm or 6mm spacers in the thirteen colors to keep some of the remaining symbolism. Alternatively, you may decide to have your thirteen primary beads be in the thirteen colors, and use pearlescent white spacers to represent Moon energy. Add a silver Moon charm and a silver bar-and-toggle clasp, and you have a lovely bracelet rosary you'll be happy to wear.

Be sure to try on the bracelet before you finish it. This may seem obvious, but it's easy to forget, especially if you're a novice beader. If your measurement wasn't quite right, you may finish the bracelet only to find it doesn't fit. Pause once you've gotten all of the beads strung and one end finished. Before you finish the second end, wrap the bracelet around your wrist for a final check. If necessary, you can still add or subtract beads to fine-tune the length. Once this is settled, you can finish the bracelet with confidence.

Hair-Dangle Rosaries

Hair-dangles can make a beautiful addition to your ritual or festival garb. They are easy to make, following the same principles of miniaturization that we used for bracelets. And best of all, hair-dangles are the most inexpensive type of rosary to make. Once you have a couple of suitable hair clips and a spool of beading wire, you can bead a new hair-dangle for no more than two or three dollars, and much less if you have a stash of seed beads on hand.

First, choose a type of hair finding (spring comb, spring clip, barrette, etc.) that stays securely in place in your hair and is pierced to accommodate a ring or clasp you can use to attach the dangle. Don't hesitate to ask your bead store to let you try on a finding to see if it will work for you and stay in your hair.

Then consider how you're going to attach the hair-dangle to the finding. If you don't expect to make more than one hair-dangle, you can, of course, attach that dangle directly to the finding, using a loop of beading wire in exactly

Figure 8-3. Hair-dangle rosaries, ready to wear.

Rosaries You Can Wear

the same way you'll attach a charm to the other end of the dangle. If you expect to make and wear more than one dangle, however, you can create an attachment that allows you to use one hair finding for all of your different dangles. The basic idea is to provide something from which the dangle can hang freely but securely. Clare's favorite method is to attach a lobster claw clasp or a spring ring to the hair finding, using a split ring or a length of beading wire and a couple of crimp beads. Since split rings can be stiff and awkward to handle unless you have a tool for opening them, she usually uses beading wire (see sidebar for detailed instructions). An attachment of this type will hold two hair-dangles together, or three if they're really light, so you're not limited to wearing one at a time.

Next, consider length. Hair-dangles, like bracelets, are short. Dangles on average should be between 3 inches and 6 inches long, unless you plan to wear them in the center back of your hair, in which case you can make them

Attaching Hair-Dangles

1. Cut a piece of beading wire about an inch long.

2. Pass the wire through the stringing loop of the lobster claw or spring ring, and then through the stringing hole of the hair finding.

3. Bend the wire so both ends are together, behind the hair finding, with the lobster claw or spring ring in front of the hair finding.

4. Put two crimp beads over the ends of the beading wire.

5. Leave a little bit of loose wire between the crimp beads and the hair finding (1/8 inch is plenty) and crush the crimp beads.

6. Snip off any excess wire and hang your hair-dangle from the lobster claw or spring ring.

in the 8 inches to 12 inches range. More than 12 inches may be too heavy for the hair finding, even if you use a lot of seed beads in the design. Gauge the length according to where you plan to place the dangle in your hair, how easily findings come loose in your hair, and comfort issues such as whether or not it will bother you to have the dangle brush your shoulder or ear when you turn your head. Also consider the length of your neck; often a short-necked person looks better with a shorter dangle, a long-necked person with a longer dangle. Here, as with the bracelet rosaries, you'll need to miniaturize your design. See the examples on the following page for some specific suggestions on hair-dangles based on designs given elsewhere in this book.

Apart from the need to miniaturize, your main design issue in making hair-dangles is the total weight of the rosary. A hair-dangle that is too heavy will pull the hair finding loose and clonk hard against your head every time you move. Therefore, think about the weight of the beads you plan to use. Beads larger than 12 to 14mm should, if possible, be light or medium weight, made from wood, bone, horn, shell, or the lighter types of metal. Stone beads should be smaller than 14mm. If you want to use a couple of really heavy beads, use seed beads to fill in the rest of the length of the dangle. Also remember that "heavy" is a relative term that needs to be considered in the context of the whole piece. Twelve stone beads of 10mm size, five of 4mm size, one of 14mm size, and an inch-long openwork metal pendant mark the upper end of the workable weight range for a hair-dangle. On the other end of the scale, you can make a lovely and very light dangle out of 6/o and 11/o seed beads and a small, light-weight metal charm. Keep in mind here the needs and comfort of the person for whom the dangle is intended, whether that's you or someone else. If the dangle turns out to be uncomfortable, it's not likely to be worn much.

Also consider whether you're going to wear your dangle a great deal—say, every couple of days, all day long—or only during rituals, in Moon lodge, or on other special occasions. You can get away with something a little long or a little heavy more easily if it's not going to be worn often. But consider, as well, whether a heavy dangle that whacks against your shoulder will distract you just when you don't want to be distracted!

Once you've considered all these factors, you're ready to make some hair-dangles. Here are sample designs to get you started:

- **Druid Four Elements hair-dangle:** 3 beads each for fire, water, air, and earth; 6 spacer beads total, one before the fire group, one between each group of three, one between the earth group and the spirit bead, and one between the spirit bead and tree charm; a spirit bead; a tree charm

- **Druid Three Realms hair-dangle:** 3 beads each for land, sea, and sky; 4 spacers; a tree charm

- **Thirteen Moons hair-dangle:** 13 beads in appropriate colors for each month; a Moon pendant

- **Triple Goddess hair-dangle:** 3 each moonstone, carnelian, and onyx beads; clear spacers as desired; spiral pendant

- Horned God hair-dangle: use three sets of bone, green glass, and wood beads as described in the original design, plus the original pendant as given

- Ancestor hair-dangle #1: mix of stone, bone, wood, horn, glass, metal beads; an animal, insect, or plant charm

- Ancestor hair-dangle #2: beads for immediate family members; suitable charm

Using Pagan Rosaries

N OW THAT YOU HAVE A PAGAN ROSARY, what do you do with it? The following practices show just a few of the many options. They are intended as examples and inspirations to you in creating your own practices.

Spells and Chants

Rosaries have commonly been used in chants, short or long, since ancient times, whether for paying reverence to a deity or calling power into a spell. A rosary can be a real advantage in spell work, since you can focus your mind completely on the words of the spell or chant and allow the movement of the beads past your hand to keep track of how many repetitions you've made.

The Song of Amergin

This ancient Irish magical poem can be used with the Thirteen Moons rosary described in chapter 7, or any other rosary with thirteen or nineteen beads or bead sets. In either case, count one bead as you recite each line in the first verse and imagine yourself as each of the images. With a thirteen-bead rosary, pause and recite all of the second verse without counting. With a nineteen-bead rosary, count one bead as you recite each question in the second verse. In either case, let answers to the questions rise in your mind.

I am a wind of the sea,
I am a wave of the sea,
I am a sound of the sea,
I am a stag of seven tines,
I am a hawk on a cliff,
I am a tear of the Sun,
I am beautiful among flowers,
I am a wild boar,
I am a salmon in a pool,
I am a lake on a plain,
I am a hill of poetry,
I am a spear that does battle,
I am a god who shapes flame into a head.
Who makes clear the ruggedness of the mountains?
Who knows where the Sun shall set?
Who knows the ages of the Moon?
Who gathers home the cattle from the house of Tethra?
Who wins a welcome from the cattle of Tethra?
Who shapes weapons from hill to hill—who but I?

Healing Chant for healing after surgery

Knit, flesh, knit,
Grow smooth and strong,
Grow straight the new
Until within
The well-healed skin
All waxes whole and true.

Ancestor Chant

Ancestors, we honor your memory.
Ancestors, we honor your lives.
Ancestors, we honor your wisdom.
Ancestors, we honor your strength.

Power Chant

My power is gathered, my power is strong;
Power from fire and power from earth
Power from water and power from air
Power from spirit, above and below.
My power is gathered, my power is strong.

Prayer

It's hard to think of anything more traditional than reciting prayers to the tactile rhythm of a rosary slipping through your fingers. Every pagan tradition,
and for that matter every pagan, has favorite ways of addressing the gods and
goddesses. The three prayers given here are meant as examples to inspire you
to come up with prayers of your own. Ceisiwr Serith's wonderful work *A Book*

of Pagan Prayer (York Beach, ME: Weiser, 2002) is full of many more ideas to suggest your own ways of speaking to deities.

Triple Goddess Prayer

Mother of us all,
You who are ever maiden
Yet bring forth all life
And wax wise in old age
Guide us, protect us,
Love us ever,
We who are your children.

Horned God Prayer

God of green life
God of red death
Hunter and hunted
Teach me the ways
Of your wilderness!

The Universal Druid Prayer (For the Four Elements Rosary)

Grant, O Spirit, thy protection
And in protection, strength
And in strength, understanding
And in understanding, knowledge
And in knowledge, the knowledge of justice
And in the knowledge of justice, the love of it
And in that love, the love of all existences
And in the love of all existences, the love of Earth, our mother, and all
    goodness.

Rituals

Ritual, of course, is one of the basic tools of pagan practice. A rosary can be used in ritual work in many different ways, and as a working tool for ritual work of various kinds. Like a wand or an *athame*, it can concentrate, direct, and dispel energies. A rosary can also be made as the focus for a particular spell, consecrated with a ritual, and then used daily with a chant to reinforce the power and intention of the spell.

Offering Ceremony

This ceremony can be changed to fit your own particular preferences —to use the name(s) of your own personal deity or deities, or to call on powers you wish to be present on the occasion. Prepare your altar in any way you wish: candles, incense, flowers, a food offering, whatever seems appropriate. Dress in whatever garments or lack of same that you prefer. Carry the strand of prayer beads in your hands. When you are ready, begin the ceremony.

1. Bright goddess, mother of all! I call upon you to offer you this gift that my hands have made. *Raise the strand up in a gesture of presentation*

2. This tool of magic is yours, even as I am yours. I dedicate it to you with love. Watch over me, guide me, in my use of these beads, even as you do in all other areas of my life. *If you are using incense, pass the strand of beads through the smoke three times. Otherwise, make a gesture of blessing over it three times. Then lay the beads on the altar. Pray, either aloud or silently, in whatever words come to you. When you are finished:* It is done. I thank you for your loving presence in my life. I thank you for all your myriad gifts.

3. *Make whatever closing gesture you wish to finish the ceremony.*

Four Elements Invocation

This ritual is an example for the Druid Four Elements rosary. Stand or sit in a natural setting, perhaps a park or garden, on a sunny day.

1. Face east, and hold your rosary by the air octad beads. Focus on the energies of air, of dawn, of spring, of childhood and youth. Feel these energies build within and around you.

2. Say the following prayer: "Powers of the east, powers of air. Bless me, I pray, and fill me with your wisdom. Help me to be ever mindful of the role you play in the world and in my life. Lead me to a greater understanding of your nature and your capacities. I thank and bless you."

3. Bow your head and feel the presence of the powers of the element of air.

4. Turn to face south and hold your rosary by the fire octad beads. Focus on the energies of fire, of noon, of summer, of young adulthood. Feel these energies build within and around you.

5. Say the following prayer: "Powers of the south, powers of fire. Bless me, I pray, and fill me with your wisdom. Help me to be ever mindful of the role you play in the world and in my life. Lead me to a greater understanding of your nature and your capacities. I thank and bless you."

6. Bow your head and feel the presence of the powers of the element of fire.

7. Turn to face west and hold your rosary by the water octad beads. Focus on the energies of water, of sunset, of autumn, of middle age. Feel these energies build within and around you.

8. Say the following prayer: "Powers of the west, powers of water. Bless me, I pray, and fill me with your wisdom. Help me to be ever

mindful of the role you play in the world and in my life. Lead me to a greater understanding of your nature and your capacities. I thank and bless you."

9. Bow your head and feel the presence of the powers of the element of water.

10. Turn to face north and hold your rosary by the earth octad beads. Focus on the energies of earth, of midnight, of winter, of old age. Feel these energies build within and around you.

11. Say the following prayer: "Powers of the north, powers of earth. Bless me, I pray, and fill me with your wisdom. Help me to be ever mindful of the role you play in the world and in my life. Lead me to a greater understanding of your nature and your capacities. I thank and bless you."

12. Bow your head and feel the presence of the powers of the element of earth.

13. Face east once again and hold your rosary by the pendant, especially by the large spirit bead. Focus on the energies of the center, of balance and harmony. Feel these energies build within and around you.

14. Say the following prayer: "Powers of the center, powers of spirit. Bless me, I pray, and fill me with your wisdom. Help me to be ever mindful of the role you play in the world and in my life. Lead me to a greater understanding of your nature and your capacities. I thank and bless you."

15. Bow your head and feel the presence of the powers of the element of spirit.

16. Sit quietly and enjoy the energies within and around you, and the beauty of the day.

Ritual of Consecration

Use this ritual with a rosary you have designed to work a particular spell. It works with the symbolism of the four elements. You will need an altar with a censer or a lit stick of incense in the east, a burning candle in the south, a cup of water in the west, a dish of salt in the east, and your new rosary in the center. You will also need to work out the purpose of the spell until you can express it in a single sentence.

Establish sacred space using whatever ritual method you prefer. If you practice Wicca, for example, cast a circle and call the quarters; if you practice Druidry in one of the Revival traditions, perform the ceremony to open a solitary grove; if you follow another tradition, use whatever ceremony it uses to begin a ritual working.

1. Go to the south side of the altar and stand facing north.

2. Lift up the rosary in both hands, offering it to the powers of earth in the north, saying: "Powers of earth, I call upon you to bless and empower this rosary with the might of the tall stones, for the fulfillment of its purpose, which is (state the purpose)."

3. Sprinkle salt over the rosary so that a few grains touch every bead. Concentrate on the image of the powers of earth flowing into the rosary.

4. Go to the east side of the altar and face west.

5. Lift up the rosary in both hands, offering it to the powers of water in the west, saying: "Powers of water, I call upon you to bless and empower this rosary with the might of the rolling waves, for the fulfillment of its purpose, which is (state the purpose)."

6. Dip your fingers into the water and sprinkle them on the rosary so that a little falls on every bead. Concentrate on the image of the powers of water flowing into the rosary.

7. Go to the north side of the altar and face south.

8. Lift up the rosary in both hands, offering it to the powers of fire in the south, saying: "Powers of fire, I call upon you to bless and empower this rosary with the might of the dancing flames, for the fulfillment of its purpose, which is (state the purpose)."

9. Move the rosary over the candle flame so that the light shines on every bead. Concentrate on the image of the powers of fire flowing into the rosary.

10. Go to the west side of the altar and stand facing east.

11. Lift up the rosary in both hands, offering it to the powers of air in the east, saying: "Powers of air, I call upon you to bless and empower this rosary with the might of the rushing winds, for the fulfillment of its purpose, which is (state the purpose)."

12. Move the rosary over the incense smoke so that the smoke touches every bead. Concentrate on the image of the powers of air flowing into the rosary.

13. Raise the rosary in both hands, offering it to the powers of spirit above you, saying: "Powers of spirit, I call upon you to bless and empower this rosary with the might of the universe itself, for the fulfillment of its purpose, which is (state the purpose)."

14. Bring the rosary to your lips and breathe gently on each bead, concentrating on the image of your breath wakening the beads to life.

15. When you are finished, say: "And with my breath I give this rosary life and power for the fulfillment of its purpose. As above, so below."

16. Put the rosary in a cloth bag and then close the ritual space, using whatever method you prefer to use.

Thereafter, once a day, take the rosary out and count each bead while repeating the purpose you have chosen. When you are not working with the rosary, try to put the spell out of your mind completely.

Meditation

Rosaries have been used for thousands of years as a help to meditation, and today's Pagan traditions have begun to make good use of this traditional practice. The examples that follow show some of the ways this can be done.

Four Elements Meditation

The eight festivals of the Druid year aren't simply arbitrary holidays; they mark out the stations of a cycle of energies and spiritual powers that can be understood and applied in many different ways. This meditation explores the stations of the year through the four elements, beginning with air, the first of the elements, and Samhuinn, the first day of the Druid year. It is performed with the Druid Four Elements rosary.

Sit in any comfortable position that keeps your spine upright and relaxed. If possible, face east to take advantage of the subtle currents of magical energy that follow the Sun's course from east to west through the sky; these help bring clarity to meditation. Your eyes should be gently open, at least for the first few times you practice this meditation. Set your rosary in your lap, holding it with your dominant hand (your right hand if you're right-handed, your left hand if you're left-handed), with your thumb and forefinger resting on the base of the feather charm, between the spirit bead and the first bead of the yellow octad of the element of air.

Take several minutes to relax your body, starting from the soles of your feet and working upward a little at a time until you reach the top of your head. Release as much tension as you can while still maintaining your posture. Once you're relaxed, turn your attention to your breathing. Breathe slowly and rhythmically, drawing your breath gently down into your abdomen. Keep your mind focused on the inflow and outflow of air through your nostrils. If you like, you can keep count of your breaths by moving one bead past thumb and forefinger with each breath, until you come around again to the spirit bead and pass it, returning to the feather charm and the starting position. Now, you're ready to begin.

1. Take hold of the first yellow bead, and think of Samhuinn (also known as Samhain or All Hallows), November 1, the beginning and end of the old Celtic calendar, the day when the spirits of the dead are free to walk the Earth once again.

2. Think of the meaning of this day in whatever tradition you follow. How does the element of air manifest in that season of the year? What are the colors of the sky and the flavor of the wind at Samhuinn? How does the element of air connect to Samhuinn's symbolism of death and rebirth?

3. Make a mental note of any images or ideas that occur to you.

4. Move your thumb and forefinger to the next bead and think of Alban Arthuan (also known as Yule or the winter solstice), December 21, the shortest day of the year, the point where the Sun ends its long retreat and turns northward again to bring warmth to the world.

5. Think of the meaning of this day according to the teachings of your own spiritual tradition. How does the element of air manifest at mid-winter? What are the skies and the wind like? What does air have to teach about the rebirth and return of the Sun?

6. In the same way, mentally explore the element of air as it expresses itself at Imbolc (Oimelc or Candlemas, February 2), Alban Eiler (Ostara or the spring equinox, March 22), Belteinne (Beltane or May Day, May 1), Alban Heruin (Litha or the summer solstice, June 22), Lughnasadh (Lammas, August 1), and Alban Elued (Mabon or the autumn equinox, September 23).

7. Make a mental note of the images, ideas, and insights that come to you.

The first time you do this meditation, one element is likely to be quite enough! In that case, proceed to the end, and pick up with the first of the fire beads at a later time. If you feel comfortable going further in one practice, however, proceed to the red beads of the octad of fire. The meditations on this octad are like those of the octad of air, starting with Samhuinn and continuing around the Wheel of the Year to Alban Elued, except that the element you're following through the seasons is fire. Bring the insights of your own spiritual tradition to bear, and don't forget the sensory lessons of the seasons themselves. The clear starlight of winter, the leaping energy of springtime growth, the hot Sun of summer, and the red leaves and wood smoke of autumn are all forms of fire, and all have much to teach you.

When you finish the octad of fire, if you feel ready to go on in this session, proceed to the first blue bead of the octad of water. Once again, the sequence of the eightfold year is your guide, but the element of water now takes center stage. Think of water in all its forms through the eight stations of the year, drawing on your own experiences of the seasons and the teachings of the tradition you follow. Then, when you finish the octad of water, if you feel ready to go on in this session, proceed to the green beads of the octad of earth and meditate on the element of earth through the eight stations of the year as before.

Finally, finish the circle and take hold of the spirit bead, turning your attention to the whole cycle in all four elements. What common themes or lessons can you find in the images, ideas, and insights that came to you in your exploration of the four elements? Explore this for a time, and then let your mind return to stillness. After a few moments, pay attention to your breathing once again, and breathe slowly and smoothly for a time before closing the meditation.

Three Realms Meditation

This meditation is for the Druid Three Realms rosary on page 110.

To begin, sit in any comfortable position that keeps your spine upright and relaxed. If possible, face east to take advantage of the subtle currents of magical energy that follow the Sun's course from east to west through the sky; these help bring clarity to meditation. Set your rosary in your lap, holding it with your dominant hand (your right hand if you're right-handed, your left hand if you're left-handed).

Take several minutes to relax your body, starting from the soles of your feet and working upward a little at a time until you reach the top of your head. Release as much tension as you can while still maintaining your posture. Once you're relaxed, turn your attention to your breathing. Breathe slowly and rhythmically, drawing your breath gently down into your abdomen, and keep your mind focused on the inflow and outflow of air through your nostrils. If you like, you can keep count of your breaths by moving one bead past your thumb and forefinger with each breath, until you come around again to the bead or charm on which you started. Now, you're ready to begin.

Bring the concept of the threshold to your mind. Turn over anything that seems to you to be connected to it. What is a threshold, anyway? Besides the part of a doorframe which crosses the floor, dividing the outdoors from the indoors or one room from another, what else might be a threshold? A division that separates one thing from another, one reality from another, one world from another? An experience, a perception, a life passage? What thresholds do we experience in daily life? Being born; achieving the ability to sit up, crawl, walk, and talk; learning to read and write, to hit a ball with a bat, or play a musical instrument; getting a first job, learning to drive, graduating from college; losing your virginity, marrying, siring or carrying and birthing a child; all of these involve crossing a threshold. Consider all of these, and anything else that comes to mind about the concept of the threshold.

The first time you do this meditation, this much material is likely to be quite enough! Stop here, therefore, unless you are an experienced meditator and are ready for more. Perhaps take some notes on what you have learned.

When you are ready to go on, take hold of your rosary by the shell charm. Be aware that, for the purposes of this meditation, this charm represents the threshold between land and sea. Meditate on what this threshold is, what it is like, what it involves, what significance it might have had to the ancient

Celtic peoples. If you wish, do some reading on this topic before beginning the meditation. Again, this may be enough for one session of meditation. If so, take some notes on what you have learned.

When you are ready to continue, repeat the meditation, but this time hold the acorn charm, and meditate on the threshold between land and sky. (A tree is one of the beings that bridges this threshold, which is why this charm is an acorn rather than a pebble or some other symbol of earth.) Again meditate on what this threshold is, and the rest of the list of topics given above. When you are finished, take notes.

Finish the circle and take hold of the feather charm, turning your attention to the threshold between sea and sky, that far horizon that haunts so many cultures both ancient and modern. Meditate upon it the same way you did upon the others. When you are finished, write down notes on what you have learned.

The fifth and last meditation is to revisit the first meditation and examine what you have learned about the nature of the threshold, of liminal space. What common themes or lessons can you find in the images, ideas, and insights that came to you in your exploration of the three realms? Explore this for a time, and then let your mind return to stillness. After a few moments, pay attention to your breathing once again, and breathe slowly and smoothly for a time before closing the meditation.

Journeying

Another important practice in today's Pagan spirituality is journeying, also known as pathworking and active imagination. This is the art of using the imagination to explore the inner worlds of mind and spirit. The examples that follow show how rosaries can be used in this work.

Three Realms Journey

This journey builds on the themes for meditation given for the Druid Three Realms rosary. It works best if you have done the meditations above before going on to the journey. Begin by learning this journey by heart, or by taping it so you can play it back to yourself. It's best not to have to use the book to read along.

Sit in a comfortable position, in a quiet place where you will not be disturbed. (You can lie down if you would be more comfortable, but make sure there's no risk that you will fall asleep.) Unplug the phone, put out the cat, shut the door. Settle down, take a deep breath, and take your rosary in your hand.

Breathe slowly and evenly in and out. Relax, let go of your tensions. Focus on your breathing. In and out. In and out. (If you tape the journey, make a 60- to 90-second pause here.) Hold your rosary by the shell charm. Imagine yourself standing in some place where land and sea meet, whether this is a rocky beach on the coast of Maine, smooth white sand in a blue Hawaiian lagoon, the long smooth grey stretch of sands along the coast of the Pacific Northwest, or some other suitable place. Feel this place as clearly as possible.

Now open yourself to the images and experiences that come to you. What do you smell, see, hear, feel? Explore this liminal space as thoroughly as you are comfortable doing. As you explore, you will see a being sitting or standing near you. What nature of being is it? Try to make a mental note of the being's appearance, so you can describe it later.

Greet the being politely. It may or may not speak to you. If it speaks, try to remember as much as possible of what it says. Feel free to enter into conversation with it, but always be polite and friendly; you are, in effect, a guest in its house. If you become uncomfortable, you can always bid it farewell and leave, bringing yourself back to the time and place where your body is located. In any case, when you are ready, thank the being for anything it may have told you, taught you, or given you.

Return to your body, to the here and now. Try to write down whatever you saw and experienced, so that you will remember it. (If you are taping the journey, make a 60- to 90-second pause here.) If you wish, you may stop the journey here and continue on another day.

Now turn the rosary in your hand so that you are holding the acorn charm. This time, imagine yourself in some place where land meets sky; a high barren hill, a snowy mountain top, a windswept moor, or some other suitable place. Feel this place as clearly as possible.

Open yourself to the images and experiences that come to you. What messages do your senses bring you, through sight, hearing, taste, smell, feeling? Explore this space as thoroughly as you are comfortable doing. As you explore, you will see a being sitting or standing near you. As always, try to make a mental note of the being's appearance, so you can write down your experience later. Greet the being politely. If it speaks to you, try to remember as much as possible of what it says. Talk freely with it, but always remember you are a guest here. If the being gives you or teaches you or tells you anything, be sure to thank it before you leave.

When you are ready, come back to an awareness of the present time and of your body.

Try to note down whatever you saw and experienced, so that you will remember it. (If you are taping the journey, make a 60- to 90-second pause here.)

If you decide to continue, turn your rosary to the feather charm. This represents the threshold between sea and sky, a boundary that seabirds constantly cross. Imagine yourself in some place where sea meets sky; perhaps out on the sea in a boat, with nothing visible from one horizon to the other except sky above and water below, or some other suitable place. Feel this place as clearly as possible.

Open yourself to the images and experiences that come to you. What messages do your senses bring you, what does your sight, hearing, sense of smell and taste, the feeling in your skin say? Explore this space as thoroughly as you are comfortable doing. As you explore, you will see a being near you. Again, try to make a mental note of the being's appearance, so you can write it down later. Greet the being politely. If it speaks to you, try to remember as much as possible of what it says. Don't hesitate to talk with it, always remaining polite as a guest should. If the being gives you or teaches you or tells you anything, be sure to thank it before you leave.

When you are ready, come back to an awareness of the present time and of your body. Try to note down whatever you saw and experienced, so that you will remember it.

The journeys finished, you are back in your own home, in your familiar life, but you bring with you new knowledge and insights. Feeling refreshed and renewed, you open your eyes. Having returned from this third journey, take a few minutes to think about everything you experienced. Realize that you can take these journeys again at any time, and that you can relive your journeys by handling the beads and charms of your rosary and letting them bring you back to these thresholds, and to the memories of your previous visits.

10

Experiencing the Moment

I JUST MISSED A BUS. The next one isn't due for fifteen minutes. I settle on the bench underneath a spreading maple tree and try to relax. My nerves are feeling frayed after a stressful workday, and it's hard to let go of the edginess this produces. I reach into my shoulder bag and work open the drawstring pouch I use to carry some of my rosaries. My fingers touch cold, smooth shapes. I pull out the first rosary that comes to my hand. By chance, it's one I use for relaxing my body and spirit, and opening my awareness. It is a long single strand, open-ended. My fingertips find the large, twelve-sided bead of red jasper that begins one end. It represents one of my patron goddesses. Slowly I trace the shape of the bead, thinking of her it represents, and of the many gifts she has brought into my life. My shoulders begin to let go. My breathing deepens. With my chattering child-mind distracted by a favorite guessing game—"I know what bead comes next!"—the deeper levels of my self begin to open.

On to the next bead, past the small glass spacer to a long, narrow bead of green bloodstone, representing a patron god. His energy blooms in all the green, growing things around me, and I thank him for the tree beneath which I sit, its tiny green flowers touching the air I am breathing with their faint scent.

More small spacers, then another long narrow stone bead, for another patron god. The end, cut at an angle, reminds me of his sudden moods, and of his immense strength. I feel that strength within my heart.

By now, I am relaxed, my muscles warming and loosening, my breathing deep and even. I move on to the next beads, each of which reminds me of an experience, a place, a person, a cherished memory. Here is the round blue-grey ceramic bead that rested in my bead box for fifteen years or more, waiting for a home, and that reminds me now of the living earth and all upon her. Further on, a silver heart with a leaf pattern chased on it is a reminder of a time of happiness and peace. A flattened yellow glass teardrop feels like sunlight taken on a solid form. A beautiful swirled blue and green glass bead, followed by a green disk: the energies and powers of water. A rectangular blue bead with stars on it connects to the everlasting sky. And other beads, glass, wood, bone, stone. At last I come to the far end, a chunky blue sodalite bead to represent another beloved patron goddess; her clarity flows through me as I touch it. A spacer, then a large bead of ocean fossil, taking me back to the seaside. Then a large clear glass bead like a raindrop, and the strand ends in a silver acorn, emblem of the seeds of new possibility.

The cares of the day forgotten, I am ready to go home and focus on the creative work awaiting me. I board the bus in a relaxed, alert state, and continue to finger the strand of beads as four big wheels carry me toward home.

I take up a strand of dark wooden beads, simply made. The purpose of this strand is to help me learn the Ogham alphabet, for it provides a symbolic language with many uses. A group of three beads hides the knot in the cord, and provides a demarcation to tell me I have finished the circuit. Their smooth surfaces slide easily between thumb and forefinger's tips as I feed them along. Then one small saucer bead: first *aicme*. More smooth wooden spheres, each separated by a single spacer bead. I recite the letter names silently to myself, calling up imagery associated with each one.

Beith, the birch of new beginnings; I see a slender white tree, upright as a candle. *Luis*, the rowan, magical protection; a bracelet of dried red berries. *Fearn* the alder, unwavering support; pillars sunk in watery mud holding up a cathedral. *Saille*, connectedness with the flow of things; a willow swaying on a riverbank. *Nuin*, the world-tree ash spanning heaven and earth, linking all together; I feel the web of connection spreading through myself and the world around me.

Now smooth curves give way to another saucer bead: second *aicme*. *Huathe*, the hawthorn, possessed of dire kennings; the strange scent of its flowers fills my nose. *Duir*, strong oaken door that either opens for opportunity or closes to shut out harm; this bead, not as round as the others, is almost acorn-shaped. *Tinne*, holly, best in the fight; a spear shaft hurtles past me in a clean, well-directed throw. *Coll*, the hazel that feeds the Salmon of Wisdom; I taste the sweetness of hazelnuts. *Quert*, the apple, emblem of the Blessed Isles; the glory of a cloud of apple blossom comes to memory.

Then the saucer of third *aicme* passes through my fingers. *Muin*, vine, distilling the wine of prophecy that is strange upon the tongue; I savor remembered wines. *Gort*, ivy twisting its slow way along an indirect path as it climbs; yet in the end it goes far, as I have so often seen. *Ngetal*, the reed, swift movement; I remember the hissing of the wind in the reeds as I stood beside what was once an abbey's fishpond. *Straif*, blackthorn, tree of necessity; the long thorns, venom-tipped, left infected wounds in my foot when stepped on unseen. *Ruis*, the Elder Mother, protectress; the flowers make a tincture that has all the freshness of Belteinne in it and I smile at the memory of that indefinably lively scent.

The fourth saucer bead brings me back to the present, and the fourth *aicme*. *Ailim*, the silver fir; I feel my back straighten at the remembrance of this tall, upright tree. *Ohn*, the gorse, a gathering of sweetness; its everpresent yellow flowers give a point to the old joke "kissing is out of season when the gorse is out of bloom." *Ur*, heather, fragrant and buzzing with bees; heather honey makes a fine mead. *Eadha*, white poplar, trembling with every wind; fear makes such a great noise over a small cause. *Ioho*, the yew spreads its evergreen canopy over English churchyards to remind all who come there that death gives way to rebirth.

The fifth saucer bead marks the transition to the final *aicme*. *Koad*, the grove, all wisdom resumed in one sacred place; the lovely mixed wild forests of the Pacific Northwest come to mind. *Oir*, the spindle tree, sudden knowledge; I see a flash of lightning, for Spindle is said to be a tree of Taranis. *Uilleand*, honeysuckle, a secret of sweetness; this letter is associated with the lapwing, a bird who hides its nest in plain sight, reminding us how many times a secret is something we have simply failed to notice. *Phagos*, the beech, books and language; I think of library shelves, smell the scent of old leather and taste the distinct dust of old books upon my tongue. *Mor*, the great sea, beginnings and endings and all great change; I stand at the seaside a moment in thought, feeling the rushing pulse of waves beating against the shore.

Then the three marker beads come to my fingers again, their angular shapes different from the smooth rounds I have been touching, reminding me that I have completed this passage through the Ogham. My memory is more deeply engraved with the order and meaning of the letters, more richly endowed with meditative associations for each *few* of this alphabet. I coil up the rosary and slip it into a pouch sewn from leaf-printed cloth, pull on the wooden beads that draw the ribbon ties of the pouch closed. The Ogham symbols and their associations remain in my mind as I go to begin preparing supper.

A friend's child has been grievously attacked by an older child. He is suffering from natural after-effects of fear and anxiety, even though his assailant has been caught and is in custody. I make a rosary for him of big, brightly colored wooden beads, seventeen of them—four yellow for air, four orange for fire, four blue for water, four black for earth, and a large white bead for spirit.

As I string the beads, I pray to several carefully chosen deities, asking them to help him learn to let go of his fear and pain, asking them to help him to clearly feel their presence when he touches the rosary. I call upon the powers of the elements as well, asking them to help him. Finally, I spray the beads with elderflower water, asking the Elder Mother to protect this innocent child. I perform a ritual of blessing over the beads and give them to my friend. He later reports that his son loves to play with the beads and takes them to bed with him at night, feeling comforted by holding them.

At about the same time that my friend's child is hurt, another friend calls to say he is soon to have major surgery. I create a healing rosary for him, choosing beads whose colors and shapes reflect the energies he will most need to heal from this particular procedure. I then go to a faery teacher he and I share, and she gives me a healing chant for him to recite when he tells the beads. I write down the chant and send both items to him, along with other gifts from a mutual friend who also wishes to help. Later, he reports that his healing is progressing well and that he can feel the chant and rosary working together to help him. I set the phone down knowing that it's experiences like these that make me truly understand the value of my rosary-making skills.

Glossary of Terms

When you first browse a bead catalog or leaf through a beading book, a bewildering list of technical terms swims before your eyes: druk, rocaille, lampwork, bugle, heishi (also spelled heishe, heshi or heshe), color-lined, millefiore, cloisonné, Delica, seed, fire-polished, AB, Iris, oil-slick, rondelle, donut, bicone, hairpipe. Some of these terms describe bead shapes, some describe bead finishes, and others describe techniques by which the beads are made. Here are the terms you are most likely to encounter.

AB: short for aurora borealis, and describes a shimmering, rainbow finish that occurs in glass beads. Any color, size, or shape of glass bead might have an AB finish. AB beads are very appealing to the eye, and have a special gleam that can really add to a piece. White or clear glass beads with an AB finish are a nice way to represent the element of spirit, to substitute for pearls in a rosary of water, or to mimic raindrops.

Barrel: long, thick beads with somewhat squared ends; think of a beer keg that has been grabbed at both ends and stretched to make it longer than it is wide. They make a good addition to an interesting mix of shapes. Some barrel beads are literally shaped like wine barrels, and these are great for deities such as Dionysus who link to wine, beer, or mead.

Bicone: a bead that is wide in the middle and narrow on both ends, like a pair of cones placed with their wide ends together. Bicone beads can also have other shaping added to them; faceted bicones and twisted bicones are commonly available, especially in glass or stone. Bicone beads are excellent choices for rosary-making. Interesting to both the eye and the hand, they work well as special beads to mark the spaces between one major bead group and another, and are a good choice for the top bead of a pendant.

Bugle: thin, very narrow glass tube beads. They are available from 2mm to about 16mm in length, in a wide range of colors, and are either smooth or faceted. Unfortunately, since bugle beads are fragile and crack or flake readily, they are not suited to most rosary making. The shorter-length bugles can be successfully used in hair-dangles.

Chicklets: rectangular beads, often made of ceramic or glass. Chicklets are a good shape to provide both visual and textural contrast for rounds, ovals, and barrels.

Cloisonné beads, properly speaking, are beads made of brightly-colored enamelwork fused to brass. The designs on them are created by using fine brass wire to shape areas for the different colors of enamel, which are then applied and fired. Most cloisonné beads currently available are simply painted with enamels, and the gold edging on the designs is also paint rather than metal. These painted beads are quite pretty and much less expensive than genuine cloisonné. Good quality cloisonné beads, whether genuine or imitation, work well in rosaries.

Color-lined: beads made of glass, with one color painted into the core of the bead to provide contrast to the color of the main body. The most common color-lined beads are seed beads, but some sources also sell larger color-lined beads. Color combinations in these beads are often quite striking; bright pale green with a dark-red core, for instance, or a pale rose-petal pink with a cobalt-blue core. Color-lined beads can make attractive and unusual additions to a rosary, especially when used as spacers.

Cylinder: thin-walled, large-holed, fairly uniform seed beads used in woven and loomed pieces and in bead embroidery. Although beautiful, they are not suited to most rosary making because they break too easily under the constant pressure created by the weight of other beads. As with bugles, however, they can work in a hair-dangle rosary.

Delica: a brand name of cylinder beads, often used without explanation in bead catalogs.

Dichroic: glass beads or pendant pieces handmade by a multi-step technique that involves fusing metal to the surface of the glass. This gorgeous glasswork is expensive ($10 to $40 for a fairly large bead), but each piece is a unique work of art, never to be repeated. As with *lampwork*, dichroic beads and pendants are heavy!

Donut: a bead shape that resembles—you guessed it—a rather thin donut. Donut beads have much larger center holes than most beads. Usually made from stone, they are beautiful beads to use as the pendant charm for a rosary. See chapter 4, page 93, for a special way to string donut pendant charms.

Druk: a technical term for round glass beads that are larger than seed beads. It comes from the Czech language. The Czech Republic is the best source for a variety of beautiful glass beads, hence the use of this term in some catalogs. Most suppliers, however, simply call these beads "rounds."

Faceted: beads that have been cut or molded to have sharply defined flat areas on their surfaces. Faceted beads have a distinctive feel and can "wake up" your sense of touch when you handle them. They also reflect light from all those extra surfaces (which is the whole point of faceting) and thus sparkle when light touches them. If you want glitz, especially if you can't afford real gold or the pricier stone beads, faceted glass beads are definitely the way to go. For top quality in faceted glass beads, Swarovski is your friend.

Fire-polished: beads with an iridescent, reflective finish that contains many colors and may appear metallic to the eye. Most fire-polished beads are also faceted. The best fire-polished beads come from the Czech Republic. These beads work wonderfully in a rosary to represent creative effort or the element of fire, or simply to give an unusual sheen to the color you have chosen.

Hairpipe: long and narrow beads, thick in the center and tapering slightly toward the ends. They tend to be approximately one to two inches long and about $1/4$ inch thick. Most hairpipe beads are made of bone, horn, or wood, and come in either natural colors or blacks, dark browns, and occasionally in dark green. Pleasant to the touch, they add a beautiful design element to a rosary, especially in the pendant.

Hank: the packaging of seed beads, consisting of several strands of beads, each usually about twelve to sixteen inches long, temporarily strung on thread. If you think about how many seed beads there are to the inch, you'll see that a hank of seed beads with four to six strands in it contains a lot of beads. If you find a seed bead you really like and expect to use it in several projects, definitely see if you can buy that bead by the hank; it saves money and gives you a good supply.

Heishi (heishe, heshi, heshe): thin, narrow beads with large holes. Remember the pukka-shell necklaces that were part of the surfer look in the '70s? The beads in those necklaces were heishi. Heishi are usually made of shell, bone, wood, or metal. Nobody agrees on how to spell the name of these beads, but lots of people use them. They work well as spacers, and shell heishi are great for a water design or to please ocean-related or water-born deities like Yemaya or Aphrodite.

Iris: also called *oil-slick*, beads with an iridescent multicolored finish. They come in colors ranging from metallic shades of silver, gold, and gunmetal, to dark blues, greens, purples, and browns. Iris seed beads make beautiful spacer beads.

Lampwork: a type of handmade glass. Many lampwork beads have one core color and splashes or splotches of other colors added on top of the basic core. Other lampwork pieces can include metal foil within the bead. Lampwork pendants are readily available in the form of leaves, flowers, fruit, faces, and animals. They are lovely, and can be a stunning addition to a rosary. Many lampwork pieces are heavy, however, so if you choose a lampwork bead remember also to choose a stronger grade of stringing material!

Luster: glass beads with a uniform, transparent shiny finish. Luster beads have a nice sheen to them and feel interesting when they slide through your fingers.

Magnifica: a brand name of cylinder bead. Like *Delica*, it's often used without explanation in bead catalogs.

Matte: beads with a dull, porous finish that may also be frosted. Although made of glass, they are exactly the opposite of sparkly; they absorb rather than reflect light. They are available in a range of unusual soft candylike colors such as cantaloupe orange, honeydew green, daffodil yellow, and rose pink. They can be a beautiful way to symbolize spring.

Millefiori: often called Venetian glass beads, made from a technique in which canes of glass are bundled together and fused to create unusual, vividly colorful designs. The name means "thousand flowers," and many millefiori beads look like flowers. As with lampwork beads, millefiori are lovely and unusual, but also quite heavy, so if you decide to use them, plan accordingly!

Oil-slick: see *Iris*.

Pony: large, colorful beads used on Native American fringe-work and in hair braiding. Large pony beads are sometimes called crow beads. Pony beads have a wide hole for their size, making them well-suited to stringing on thicker cords. Kids love pony beads! So do seniors with poor eyesight or arthritis, because pony beads are easy to see and handle, and they come in bright colors.

Potato: unevenly-shaped oval beads. These are usually found as glass, freshwater pearl, or mother-of-pearl beads. Their unusual, unpredictable shapes are fun to work into a design and catch the attention when your fingers touch them.

Rice: are like small potato beads, with the same advantages. They are most often available as freshwater or cultured pearl beads.

Rocaille is used in most bead books and catalogs to designate seed beads which have large square stringing holes that are lined with silver foil. These beads catch the light and glow from within, giving gorgeous color and light to a piece. They make excellent spacer beads. However, in the Czech Republic, all seed beads are *rocailles* and some catalogs follow this usage. If you want silver-lined seed beads and you are ordering from a catalog or Web site, double-check to be sure you get what you want.

Roller: pony or crow beads, usually made out of opaque glass.

Rondelle beads look like fat little donuts with average-sized holes and a fairly even thickness from center to edge. Some beads described as rondelles are thin at the edges, but that is more properly described as a saucer.

Saucer: similar to rondelles, but with thin edges and a thick center instead of a uniform thickness.

Seed beads: small beads that look like seeds. They are sold by size. The sizes commonly available range from 6/o (approximately eight beads to the inch) to 16/o (approximately 28 beads to the inch). Most seed beads are not perfectly uniform in size, so the number of beads per inch will vary a bit. Japanese and Czech seed beads use different size scales, adding to the complications. Generally speaking, the larger seed beads

Pagan Prayer Beads

(6/o and 8/o) make excellent spacer beads in rosary making but the smaller beads are somewhat too small. The exceptions to this are hair-dangles or small pocket rosaries on the one hand, and on the other hand, a special technique of stringing donut beads or other unusual pendant beads, given in chapter 4. In these instances, size 10/o or 11/o are also good choices. Smaller than 11/o, however, really is too small to be useful for rosary making. Some suppliers also carry larger sizes of seed beads (1/o, 2/o, 4/o, and the confusingly numbered 33/o, which is the largest of all). These are suitable for primary beads in a rosary, or to use as large spacers.

Silver-lined or *S/L*: see *rocaille*.

Strand: a single string of beads, temporarily strung. The strand is to the larger bead what the hank is to the seed bead—a way of buying a bunch of the same style of bead for a lower price than you would pay if you bought them individually. Strands vary in length and in the number of beads they contain. A strand of glass beads often contains 25 beads and is only six to ten inches long, but a strand of tumbled amber nuggets may contain 32 beads and be sixteen inches long. A strand of bone beads may contain 99 beads and be twenty-four to thirty inches long. Strands also vary quite a bit in price. A strand of 25 glass beads may cost $2, a strand of bone beads about $12, and a strand of amber nuggets $90. Like hanks, strands are the way to go if you find a bead you will need in larger numbers. You may occasionally find a strand of seed beads, especially in the larger sizes of 6/o or 8/o, and these are also usually a good bargain, giving you sixteen inches of beads for as little as $1.50. (These prices are as of Fall 2006.)

Twisted: glass beads that have been given a slight twist during the making. This unusual shape is beautiful to the eye and pleasant to the hand. Where faceted beads "wake up" the hand with their sharpness, twisted beads are wonderfully smooth and flow softly through your fingers. In addition to the beauty of their shape, many twisted beads come in unusual colors, sometimes a single bead combining a soft cloud of darker color in its heart with a lighter-colored outer body.

White-heart: beads made of two layers of glass—a central layer of opaque white glass and an outer layer of transparent colored glass.

Suppliers

Bead Studio
266 East Main Street
Ashland, OR 97520
541-488-3037
www.beadstudio.com

Fire Mountain Gems & Beads
1 Fire Mountain Way
Grants Pass, OR 97526-2373
800-423-2319 customer service
800-355-2137 order line (24/7)
www.firemountaingems.com

Garden of Beadin'
PO Box 1535
Redway, CA 95560
800-232-3588 customer service
800-BEAD-LUV order line
www.gardenofbeadin.com

Shipwreck Beads
8560 Commerce Place Drive NE
Lacey, WA 98516
800-950-4232
www.shipwreck.com

TSI
101 Nickerson Street
Seattle, WA 98109
800-426-9984
www.tsijeweltools.com
(tools & findings only; $25 minimum order)

Bibliography

Bateman, Sharon. *Findings and Finishings*. Loveland, CO: Interweave Press, 2003.

Best, Michael R., and Frank H. Brightman, eds. *The Book of Secrets of Albertus Magnus*. Oxford: Oxford University Press, 1973.

Crowley, Aleister. *777*. York Beach, ME: Weiser, 1973.

Durant, Judith, and Jean Campbell. *The New Beader's Companion*. Loveland, CO: Interweave Press, 2005.

Greer, John Michael. *Encyclopedia of Natural Magic*. St. Paul, MN: Llewellyn, 2000.

Kanan, Debbie. *The Basics of Bead Stringing*. Santa Monica, CA: Borjay Press, 2001.

McLean, Adam, ed. *The Magical Calendar*. Grand Rapids, MI: Phanes, 1994.

Musante, Lynda S. and Maria Given Nerius. *Jewelry Making for Fun & Profit*. Roseville, CA: Prima Publishing, 2000.

Rempel, Karen. *Complete Beading for Beginners*. Madeira Park, BC: Harbour Publishing, 1996.

Serith, Ceisiwr. *A Book of Pagan Prayer*. York Beach, ME: Weiser, 2002.

Spears, Therese. *Flash Jewelry Making and Repair Techniques*. Boulder, CO: Promenade Publishing, 1990.

Wiley, Eleanor, and Maggie Oman Shannon. *A String and a Prayer: How to Make and Use Prayer Beads*. York Beach, ME: Red Wheel/Weiser, 2002.

About the Authors

JOHN MICHAEL GREER is the Grand Archdruid of the Ancient Order of Druids in America and a widely respected writer and teacher. He has been a student of the occult traditions and nature spirituality for more than twenty-five years. He began following the Druid path in 1993 with initiation into the Order of Bards, Ovates, and Druids, where he has been honored with awards and elected offices. Greer is the author of numerous articles and books, including *The Druidry Handbook* (Weiser, 2006), and he is co-author of *Learning Ritual Magic* (Weiser, 2004). Greer lives in Ashland, Oregon, with his wife where he can be found blogging at *http://www.thearchdruidreport.com*.

CLARE VAUGHN is a long-time beader as well as a priestess and ceremonial magician. She is the Archdruid of the Fire and an archpriestess of the Ancient Order of Druids in America. She is an Ovate in OBOD and holds ordination through the pagan arm of the Universal Gnostic Church, and is a founding member of two magical lodges. She has done beadwork for more than fifteen years. Her interest turned to prayer beads in 2003, and since then she has made dozens of strands. Her own personal practice includes extensive use of pagan rosaries and prayer beads. Vaughn is the co-author of *Learning Ritual Magic* (Weiser, 2004). She lives in Ashland, Oregon where she maintains a prayer bead log at *http://www.clare-vaughn.livejournal.com*.